Complete this questionnaire for your [
of Dylon Multi-Purpose Dye

In order to help increase our awareness of our customer [
complete the following questionnaire. In return we will s
Multi-Purpose Dye. Many thanks for your time.

CW00348039

Name:

Address:

Telephone (daytime):

☐ Male   ☐ Female

Age group: ☐ 16-24   ☐ 25-34   ☐ 35-49   ☐ 50-64   ☐ 65 and over

Occupation:

Have you used Dylon before? ☐ Yes   ☐ No

What do you like/dislike about Dylon?

Which Dylon dyes have you used?

☐ *Multi-Purpose Dye*   ☐ *Cold Water Dye*
☐ *Hand Dye*   ☐ *Machine Dye*

What do you mainly use Dylon for?

☐ Fabric   ☐ Craft   ☐ Other (please state):

What types of magazines do you usually purchase/read?

Craft (eg *Creative Crafts*):

Lifestyle (eg *House Beautiful*):

Womens Interest (eg *Hello*):

Fashion (eg *Cosmopolitan*):

Other (please specify):

Where do you usually purchase Dylon dyes?

☐ Supermarket   ☐ Department Store   ☐ Woolworths   ☐ DIY/Hardware   ☐ Craft
☐ Haberdashery   ☐ Other

Would you like information about our Dylon Fabric Care Range of products?

☐ Yes   ☐ No

Please indicate your colour preference for your free sample of *Dylon Multi-Purpose Dye*:
(please tick one box)

☐ Carnival (Bright Pink) #13   ☐ Tangerine (Orange) #39   ☐ Kingfisher (Aqua Blue) #33

PLEASE RETURN TO: MARKETING DEPARTMENT, DYLON INTERNATIONAL LTD, WORSLEY
BRIDGE ROAD, LOWER SYDENHAM, LONDON SE26 5HD

First published in this paperback edition 1999
by Guild of Master Craftsman Publications Ltd
Castle Place, 166 High Street, Lewes,
East Sussex BN7 1XU

Produced by Tracy Marsh Publications Pty Ltd
P.O. Box 116, Henley Beach, 5022 South Australia
Tel: (08) 8355 4716; Fax: (08) 8355 4916

Publisher: **Tracy Marsh**
Publishing Manager: **Jane Moseley**
Designer: **Vanessa Byrne**
Editor: **Leonie Draper**
Dylon Advisers: **Amanda Healey & Clare Letherbarrow**
Stylist: **Georgina Dolling**
Photographer: **Joe Filshie**
Production Director: **Mick Bagnato**

ISBN 186108 157 X

Manufactured by Phoenix Offset, Hong Kong
Printed in Hong Kong

Whilst all care is taken to provide the reader with knowledge of the safety
precautions and techniques relating to the use of the materials featured
in this book, neither the Publisher, nor the Producer can take responsibility
for personal injury or mishap which may occur while working with the materials.
Please read carefully all manufacturer's instructions regarding the safe
and effective use of materials and equipment before commencing work.
Note: colours shown throughout the book are inevitably different from
true life colours as a result of the printing process.

CREATING
COLOUR
WITH DYLON

Guild of Master Craftsman Publications Ltd

Introduction

I have always been excited by colour and using dye. In particular, I love the way in which it changes the feel and mood of different materials. So I was absolutely delighted when I was asked by Dylon to write the introduction to this excellent book. Not only is it filled with lots of new and unusual ways of using dyes, but it has all the practical information you could ever need for foolproof dyeing. The book is clearly set out, just like a cookery book, with a highlighted materials and equipment list for each project. Dotted throughout are tips and ideas for improved and easy dyeing. What a joy, a workbook that is compact and easy to use.

There are lots of home craft projects, including ideas for wood and fabric as well as more traditional ones, revisited with a modern twist. The great thing about most of these projects is that they are quick, easy to achieve and do not need an investment in expensive equipment. For those of you who have a wider interest in crafts, there are clear guidelines on dyeing more unusual items such as grasses, flowers, even candles. I found particularly charming the long-eared rabbit on page 60 which has been given the washed-out, faded look of old cloth, so it resembles a genuine heirloom. And you can achieve the same, just by the use of Koala Brown Cold Water Dye.

Whether your interest is in home interiors or pure craft, this has to be the book for you!

Juliet Bawden

Contents

Working with Colour

Dyeing is an inexpensive and effective way to have the entire rainbow of colours to work with, whether you're redesigning to create a colour co-ordinated living space or simply adding new vibrancy to existing items.

Three ways you can work with colour are to:

- co-ordinate similar colours, eg pair blues with purples;
- contrast colours for dramatic effect, eg team tangerine with emerald green;
- graduate shades of the same colour, working from the palest lilac to the deepest violet.

Whichever ways you choose to work with colours, dyeing is a fantastic method of colouring in your world.

Colour Effects

Before deciding on a colour scheme to work with there are a few important tips to bear in mind.

Mood

Colours create their own particular mood. Bright vibrant colours tend to be invigorating and cheerful. Deep intense colours can create a contemplative feel. Consider the appropriate mood for your needs when choosing colours.

Surroundings

Different levels of light can alter the appearance of colours. In a room with low natural light levels your carefully selected combination of deep purple, navy blue and charcoal grey may all end up looking indistinguishable from one another. In a brightly lit area some colours will look washed out and faded, even when newly dyed.

Raw Materials

The same colour dye, when used on different materials, can give many varied colours. This is true even of things dyed in the same batch of dye mix. For example, a densely woven fabric will retain much more colour than an open weave fabric, so although they may both bathe in the same solution for the same length of time, the results will not be identical. Differing textures will also yield varied colour results.

Once you realise this you can use it to good effect, creating subtle variations around your chosen colours. Use the same colour on timber pieces, on fabric furnishings, and on flowers all in the one room and the effect will be stunning: varied yet harmonious.

Designing Colour Schemes

When it comes to choosing colours for simple dyeing projects, eg candles or pegs, if you are not satisfied with your colour choices it is not too great a problem. However, if you've selected and dyed metres of materials it can be very disconcerting to find you're not happy with your colour choices.

There are a few simple guidelines to help with this. Refer to contemporary magazines to get a feel for the way different colours work together. Or better still, go window shopping and see what colours expert designers are combining. It's a good idea to then dye small samples of your materials (or the insides or underneath of solid pieces) to check that the combinations you have in mind will work.

You may become very adventurous and mix dye colours to create unique shades. If so, be sure to keep a record of these recipes and test the new colour on a piece of scrap before starting on the actual dyeing.

Most importantly, use your imagination and have fun working with dyes to create the exact look which you desire for your wardrobe, your decor, or for a whole range of useful items.

Equipment

You will readily find most of the equipment you will need to work with about the home. To get started you will need:

Dye bath—for large dyeing projects you will need a container large enough to hold your material and to allow room for it to move freely in the mixture. Ensure the container is non-porous and large enough to allow you to agitate the material freely during dyeing.

Mixing jug or bowl—glass or stainless steel are best as they do not retain the colour. They should be large enough to hold about 500mls of liquid.

Paint brushes & sponges—you will need various size paint brushes and sponges depending on the project.

Paper towel—paper towel is perfect for drying small dyed craft items on.

Protective sheet—use newspaper or an old drop sheet to protect your work surface when dyeing.

Rubber gloves—you will need these to protect your hands.

Scales & glass, boil-proof measuring jug, measuring spoons—these are required for measuring dye powders, solutions and fabric.

Sieve—for dipping your project into the dye bath, a sieve will be needed. See Lima Bean project on page 56 as an example.

Stirring utensil—you will need an implement to stir the solutions. Use an old wooden spoon or fork or a glass rod.

Dyeing Techniques

There are four different types of dye: *Dylon Cold Water Dye, Dylon Multi-Purpose Dye, Dylon Hand Dye* and *Dylon Machine Dye.* Your choice of dye will depend on the project you decide to do and particular effect you are trying to achieve.

The table on page 13 details the many and varied uses of the four Dylon dyes. It is a useful reference for purchasing the appropriate dye.

Dylon Cold Water Dye

This dye is designed for hand dyeing with cold water. It is perfect for dyeing small fabric items and with *Dylon Cold Dye Fix* gives permanent vibrant colour to natural fabrics including cotton, linen and viscose; lighter shades will be achieved on wool and silk. For craft projects, it is suitable for wood, candles, paper, grains and beans.

Dylon Multi-Purpose Dye

This is a non-colourfast dye and is ideal for small fabric articles and various craft projects. It is specially formulated to dye nylon and garments containing Lycra® elastane as well as natural fabrics including cotton, linen, viscose, wool and silk. For craft projects, it is suitable for wood, wicker, paper, feathers, raffia, dried flowers and grasses.

Dylon Hand Dye

This dye is designed for hand dyeing with hottest tap water. It gives vibrant and colourfast colours to cotton, linen and viscose; lighter shades will be achieved on polycotton, wool and silk.

Dylon Machine Dye

This dye is good for dyeing larger items and was used for the lime green cushion on page 6. Full shades of the colour are obtained on cotton, linen and viscose. Only use clean, stain free fabrics without special finishes.

9

Dyeing Fabric

When dyeing fabric it is important to follow the instructions that come with the chosen dye.

The following instructions are for 250gms of dry weight fabric (500gms for *Dylon Machine Dye*). Adjust dye quantities, water, salt and any fixatives accordingly if dyeing larger quantities of fabric.

Dylon Cold Water Dye

INSTRUCTIONS

1. Weigh, wash, rinse article and leave damp.
2. Wearing rubber gloves, pierce tin and dissolve powder in 500mls of hot water, stirring well.
3. Add solution to container (dye bath or stainless steel sink depending on size of article) with enough cold water to cover article.
4. For each tin of dye dissolve 125gms salt and one sachet of *Dylon Cold Dye Fix* in hot water and add to dye bath, stirring well.
5. Put in clean damp article and dye for one hour, stirring constantly for the first ten minutes and then occasionally for the next 50 minutes. Keep article submerged.
6. Rinse in cold water until water runs clear and then wash separately in very hot water and washing detergent to remove any dye residue. Dry away from direct sunlight.

See special instructions for wool and A52 Black.

NOTE: WASH ARTICLE SEPARATELY FOR FIRST FEW WASHES TO REMOVE EXCESS DYE.

Dylon Multi-Purpose Dye

INSTRUCTIONS

1. Weigh, wash, rinse article and leave damp.
2. Fill saucepan/container with enough hot water to cover article.
3. Wearing rubber gloves, dissolve dye in 500mls of boiling water and stir well.
4. Add solution to saucepan/container with 30gms salt, stirring well.
5. Insert clean, damp article and raise temperature to simmer. Stir constantly for 20 minutes.
6. Rinse article until water runs clear. Results are not colourfast, so dyed garments should be turned inside out and washed separately.

Dylon Hand Dye

1. Weigh dry article and wash even if new. Leave damp.
2. Wearing rubber gloves, empty contents of the dye packet into a 1 litre/2 pint container. Stir in a small amount of warm water to form a paste and then gradually add warm water to the 1 litre mark. Dissolve thoroughly.
3. Fill dye bath with 6 litres/12 pints of hottest tap water (60°C).
4. Add 250gms of salt and stir to dissolve. Add the dye solution and stir well.
5. Place damp, unfolded article in dye bath and dye for one hour. Agitate for first 15 minutes by squeezing the dye through article and lifting out of the dye solution to prevent folds forming. Repeat stirring action at regular intervals for next 45 minutes, keeping the article submerged.
6. Rinse article in cold water until water runs clear. Wash separately in hot water with washing detergent.
7. Dry article away from direct heat and sunlight.

NOTE: ALTHOUGH THE COLOUR IS NOW COLOURFAST, WASH FABRIC SEPARATELY FOR FIRST FEW WASHES TO REMOVE EXCESS DYE.

Dylon Machine Dye

INSTRUCTIONS

1. Weigh dry article. Wash with usual detergent without conditioner and leave damp.
2. Empty contents of pack into dry drum (not soap dispenser) .
3. Add 500gms/1lb of salt, covering area where dye was added. Put in damp unfolded fabric.
4. Run 60°C colourfast cotton cycle without pre-wash.
5. When programme is finished, add wash powder and run through complete hottest programme for the garment, 95°C if possible.
6. Dry away from sunlight and direct heat. Do not tumble dry.

Dyeing Wood

Both *Dylon Cold Water Dye* and *Dylon Multi-Purpose Dye* can be used to dye wood. The coverage and final results are very similar—select dye according to colour required.

In addition to the equipment list on page 8, you will need the following when dyeing wood: fine grade sandpaper, methylated spirits (for use with *Dylon Cold Water Dye*) and varnish.

Dylon Cold Water Dye

INSTRUCTIONS

1. Rub down to bare wood and clean thoroughly. Ensure there is no varnish, or other special finish, remaining on the wood.
2. Wearing rubber gloves, pierce dye tin and dissolve dye in 250mls of warm water. Add 250mls of methylated spirits and stir well.
3. Working on a protected surface, apply colour to wooden surface with a paint brush or sponge. Allow to dry thoroughly on paper towel.
4. Apply further coats to achieve density of colour desired, allowing each coat to dry before applying the next one.
5. Allow to dry thoroughly and apply a coat of clear varnish. When dry, lightly sand and varnish again.

Dylon Multi-Purpose Dye
Follow instructions as for *Dylon Cold Water Dye* but at step 2 dissolve dye in 500mls of hot water and DO NOT add methylated spirits.

Dyeing Other Items

Both *Dylon Cold Water Dye* and *Dylon Multi-Purpose Dye* can be used to dye a range of interesting items. See the individual projects pages 44 onwards for instructions on dyeing other surfaces.

Category	Cold Water Dye	Multi-Purpose Dye	Hand Dye	Machine Dye
Fabric				
Acrylic	◆	◆	◆	◆
Canvas	★★★★	★★★★	★★★★	★★★★
Cotton	★★★★	★★★★	★★★★	★★★★
Linen	★★★★	★★★★	★★★★	★★★★
Lycra	◆	★★★	◆	◆
Nylon	◆	★★★★	◆	◆
Nylon/Polyester	◆	★★	◆	◆
Polyester	◆	◆	◆	◆
Polyester/Cotton	★★	★★	★★	★★
Silk	★★	★★★★	★★★	◆
Viscose	★★★★	★★★★	★★★★	★★★★
Viscose/Rayon	★★★★	★★★★	★★★★	★★★★
Wool	★★	★★★	★★	◆
Wood	★★★	★★★★	◆	◆
Candles	★★★★		◆	◆
Wicker		★★★★	◆	◆
Paper	★★★★	★★★★	◆	◆
Feathers		★★★	◆	◆
Raffia		★★★★	◆	◆
Lima Beans	★★★★	★★★★	◆	◆
Chick Peas	★★★★	★★★★	◆	◆
Dried Flowers		★★★★	◆	◆

Key

★★★★ Full strength colour
★★★ Full strength colour however, follow specific instructions
★★ Good results but not full strength colour
★ Pastel shades
◆ Do not dye

NOTE: DO NOT DYE FABRICS WITH SPECIAL FINISHES (EG DRIP-DRY AND 'DRY CLEAN ONLY' TYPES)

STAINS, FADED AREAS AND BLEACH CANNOT BE COVERED WITH DYE

Fabulous Fabrics

Muslin Drapes

These soft and pretty pastel drapes will add a delicate sophisticated touch to any room.

Method

Weigh the dry fabric in batches according to the required colours. You will need to use one tin of dye for every 250gms of dry weight fabric. Each tin of dye requires one sachet of *Dylon Cold Dye Fix* and 125gms salt.

Follow the instructions given on page 10 for dyeing fabrics with *Dylon Cold Water Dye*. Wash the muslin lengths and leave them damp. Mix up the dye solutions and use each one in turn to dye the required lengths of muslin. Be sure to agitate the muslin thoroughly for the required time to ensure even colouring. Rinse the fabric and hang it to dry.

The finished lengths can be made up into proper curtains or can be draped over curtain rods to give an exotic air to a room.

Materials
- *Dylon Cold Water Dyes*: Moon Blue (A06); Primrose (A10)
- *Dylon Cold Dye Fix*
- salt
- muslin lengths

Equipment
- scales
- dye bath
- rubber gloves
- glass jug
- stirring utensil

 Tip
An alternative way to open the tin of dye is to prise the edges up with a bottle opener and lift the lid off.

Materials
- *Dylon Hand Dye*:
  Deep Pink (29) (for Cushion
  & Chair Cover)
- *Dylon Cold Water Dye*:
  Purple Vine (A19) (for
  Lampshade)
- *Dylon Cold Dye Fix*
- salt
- lampshade
- cushion cover
- cushion insert
- homespun cotton fabric
- braided cord

Equipment
- scales
- dye bath
- rubber gloves
- glass jug
- stirring utensil
- sponge
- protective sheet
- permanent markers

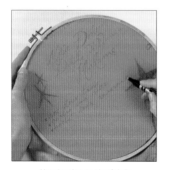

*Hand write on the fabric
with Dylon Color Fun Pens or paint.*

Scripted Fabric

After the fabrics have been dyed, you can create a stunning script effect with a metallic pen.

Method for Lampshade
Ensure the lampshade is clean and free from dust or stains. Wearing rubber gloves, pierce tin of *Dylon Cold Water Dye* and dissolve in 500mls of hot water. For each tin of dye dissolve 125gms salt and one sachet of *Dylon Cold Dye Fix* in hot water and add to solution. Stir well and allow dye solution to cool.

Working on a protected surface, dip the sponge in the dye solution and squeeze it out slightly so it does not drip dye. Wipe the sponge over the lampshade in panels from top to bottom. Even out any colour variations as you apply the second coat by gently rubbing the sponge in a circular motion.

Method for Cushion and Chair Cover
Weigh the dry fabric. You will need to use one packet of dye and 250gms of salt for every 250gms of dry weight fabric.

Follow the instructions given on page 11 for dyeing fabrics with *Dylon Hand Dye*. Wash the cushion cover and fabric and leave them damp. Mix up the dye solutions and dye the fabrics. If there is room in your dye bath you can dye them simultaneously. Be sure to agitate the fabrics thoroughly for the required time to ensure even colouring. The denser of the two fabrics should come out of the dye bath earlier as it will absorb a deeper colour. Rinse the fabric and hang it to dry.

Once the pieces are dry, apply your chosen design. We have drawn on a pattern using a gold metallic pen but you could also get a fabulous effect from fabric paints.

Bedroom Set

*Co-ordinate and contrast colours to give
a beautiful bedroom look.*

Materials
- *Dylon Hand Dyes*: Yellow (01); Royal Blue (26)
- salt
- cotton sheet, pillow case & duvet cover

Equipment
- scales
- dye bath
- rubber gloves
- glass jug
- stirring utensil
- pegs or bulldog clips
- string or elastic bands

Method
Interesting effects can be achieved with a single colour dye by using either a clamping technique (bulldog clip or peg) or a tying technique (elastic or string). The clamped or tied area resists the absorption of dye and creates a pattern.

Clamping: Fold the fabric in concertina pleats to form a long thin strip. Clip pegs or bulldog clips at intervals along the strip, either in line with the edge of the fabric fold or at an angle.

Tying: To create stripes across the fabric, fold the pieces into a thin strip of concertina pleats. Bind the piece tightly at regular intervals using string or elastic bands.

You will need to use one packet of dye and 250gms of salt for every 250gms of dry weight fabric.

Follow the instructions given on page 11 for dyeing fabrics with *Dylon Hand Dye*. Wash the bed linen and while it is still damp fold and bind as described above. Mix up the dye solutions and dye the bed linen. Be sure to agitate the pieces thoroughly for the required time so that the dye is absorbed evenly. Rinse the pieces thoroughly.

When the water is nearly running clear, remove the bindings and continue to rinse out excess dye. When the water is completely clear, wash the fabric in hot water with normal washing powder to remove any remaining dye. Hang the bed linen to dry.

Dye the fabric after clamping with bulldog clips.

 Tip
You could dye plain lengths of fabric then make up into sheets, pillow cases and duvet covers to suit your bed.

Materials

- *Dylon Hand Dyes*: Yellow (01); Royal Blue (26); Deep Pink (29); Cherry Red (36); Green (59)
- salt
- cotton clothing

Equipment

- scales
- dye bath
- rubber gloves
- glass jug
- stirring utensil

Clothing

Bring new life to clothing when dyed in the latest fashion colours.

Method

Weigh the dry fabric in batches according to the required colours. You will need to use one packet of dye and 250gms of salt for every 250gms of dry weight fabric.

Follow the instructions given on page 11 for dyeing fabrics with *Dylon Hand Dye*. Wash the clothing and leave damp. Mix up the dye solutions and use each one in turn to dye the required colour. Be sure to agitate the clothing thoroughly for the required time to ensure even colouring. Rinse the shirts and hang them on padded clothes hangers to dry to avoid marking during drying.

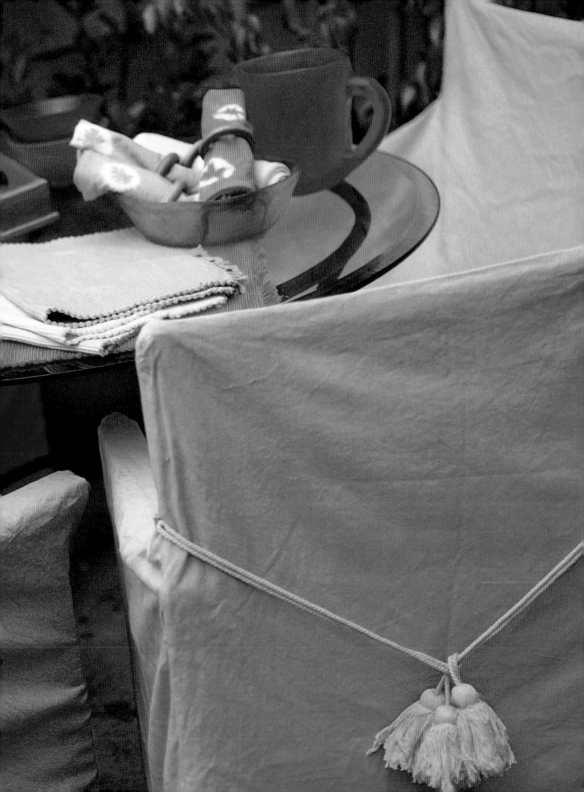

Materials

- *Dylon Cold Water Dyes*: Nasturtium (A18); Mexican Red (A21); Bahama Blue (A23); Leaf Green (A24)
- *Dylon Cold Dye Fix*
- salt
- fabric serviettes & placemats
- chair covers & cords

Equipment

- scales
- dye bath
- rubber gloves
- glass jug
- stirring utensil
- rice grains (for serviettes)
- string or elastic bands (for serviettes)

Make small pouches of rice scattered over the serviettes.

Tip
Swap the cords around so that you have colours which contrast with the chair covers.

Outdoor Setting

Combine summer colours to brighten up your outdoor setting.

Method for Placemats and Chair Covers

Weigh the dry placemats, chair covers and cords in batches according to the required colours. You will need to use one tin of dye for every 250gms of dry weight fabric. Each tin of dye requires one sachet of *Dylon Cold Dye Fix* and 125gms salt.

Follow the instructions given on page 10 for dyeing fabrics with *Dylon Cold Water Dye*. Wash all the pieces and leave them damp. Mix up the dye solutions and use each one in turn to dye the required pieces. Be sure to agitate the fabric for the required time to ensure even colouring. Rinse the dyed pieces thoroughly. Continue rinsing until water runs clear. Hang all the pieces to dry.

Method for Serviettes

Create the patterned effect on the serviettes by making a pouch of fabric, pouring a few grains of dry rice into the pouch and tightly binding it with string or elastic. Scatter the pouches over the serviette.

Follow the instructions above for dyeing placemats and chair covers and the instructions on page 10 for dyeing fabrics with *Dylon Cold Water Dye.*

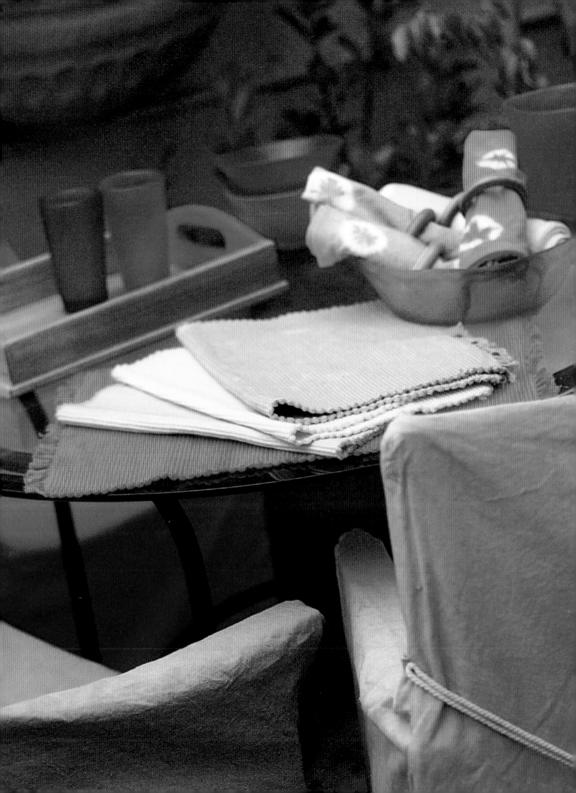

Materials

- *Dylon Hand or Machine Dyes*: Yellow (01); Deep Pink (29); Deep Violet (30); Green (59)
- salt
- towels

Equipment

- scales
- rubber gloves
- glass jug

Towels

Transform old towels, hand towels and face cloths with bright fresh colours

Method

Weigh the dry towels in batches according to the required colours.

Follow the instructions given on page 11 and 12, for dyeing fabrics with *Dylon Hand and Machine Dyes*. Wash the towels and leave them damp and unfolded. You will need to use one pack of *Dylon Hand Dye* for every 250g of dry weight fabric—ideal for hand towels and face cloths. For heavier items such as bath towels use *Dylon Machine Dye*, which will dye up to 500g of fabric.

With *Dylon Hand Dye* be sure to agitate the towels thoroughly for the required time to ensure even colouring. Rinse the towels and hang them to dry.

Towels which have some form of trim within them or on the edges will give especially interesting results as the different fabric types will absorb the dyes at varying intensities.

Materials

- *Dylon Cold Water Dyes*:
  Lilac (A03); Sahara Sun
  (A22); Ultra Violet (A26);
  Turquoise Saga (A30)
- *Dylon Cold Dye Fix*
- salt
- 6m white homespun cotton
- 4m backing fabric
- 2m x 1.5m wadding

Equipment

- scales
- spray bottle
- rubber gloves
- glass jug
- stirring utensil
- invisible & matching thread
- sewing machine
- large safety pins

Diagram 1　　　*Diagram 2*

Diagram 3

Quilt

The delicate pattern in this quilt is created by spray dyeing the fabric.

Method

Quilt size approximately 150cm x 200cm.

Tear the fabric into lengths: two x 65cm, one x 90cm, one x 1.70m. Tear the long sides of the remaining 2m into two lengths—one x 48cm and one x 60cm. Machine wash with usual detergent. Spin dry lightly, until the fabric is just damp.

Working on a protected surface, mix the dyes according to the instructions on page 10—using a ratio of one tin of dye to 1 pint/500ml of water.

Spread one 65cm length and the 48cm length flat on the newspaper and spray them evenly yellow. Spray a 65cm length pale mauve. Spray the 1.70m piece turquoise (this includes enough fabric for the binding). Spray the 90cm length and the 60cm length dark purple. These are for the borders. Allow fabric to dry completely. Rinse thoroughly until water runs clear. Dry fabric out of direct sunlight and heat and then iron.

Take the yellow fabric and fold selvedge to selvedge and then fold again in the same direction. Lay the folded fabric flat on the table, trim the edge, and then cut five strips each 12cm wide. Cut these strips into 12cm squares and again across the diagonal to make triangles. Fold and cut the pale mauve fabric in the same way.

Fold and cut the dark mauve fabric into 6.5cm strips and then into 17cm rectangles. Trim one end of each rectangle to a 45° angle. Fold and cut the turquoise fabric in the same way.

Sew each yellow triangle to a mauve triangle (see diagram 1). When these are all sewn, sew a turquoise rectangle to one side of each square. Sew a dark purple rectangle to the other side of each square (see diagram 2). Fold the corner to sew the 45° angle seam. Press each square carefully without stretching the sides.

Join four of these sections into a larger square turning the block each time 90 degrees (see diagram 3). Sew three and a half of these blocks together to make the first section of the quilt and sew five and a half sections in a line to make the quilt. Press the finished quilt top.

Cut four 12cm strips of yellow border fabric and sew to the sides of the quilt and then to the top and bottom edges. Cut 15cm strips of dark purple fabric and sew these to the sides, top, and bottom. Press well.

Cut the backing fabric in half and join together, press seam. Lay flat on a table and put the two pieces of wadding on top, place the quilt top on this and, using safety pins, pin the quilt layers together securely.

Machine quilt using either a matching thread or an invisible thread in the top, sew through all layers around the stitching lines in the blocks.

Cut a 9cm wide binding from the remaining turquoise fabric and join two strips together. Fold in half lengthwise and sew the binding to the edges of the quilt with both cut edges together. Sew all four sides and then fold the binding to the back of the quilt and hand stitch in place.

Wonderful Wood

Wooden Boxes

These simple balsa wood boxes can be dyed to suit every decor. Try a colourful Mexican combination.

Method

Rub down to bare wood and clean thoroughly, ensuring there is no varnish or special finish on the wood. Wearing rubber gloves, pierce dye tins and dissolve dye according to instructions on page 12 for dyeing wood with *Dylon Multi Purpose Dye* and *Dylon Cold Water Dye*.

Working on a protected surface, brush the dye on the outside of the lids and boxes. Allow to dry on paper towel before brushing dye on the insides. Apply as many coats as needed to achieve the required colour.

Seal with a spray sealer and allow to dry. Varnish the outside of each box and lid. Allow to dry. Lightly sand and varnish again.

You can further decorate the boxes by adding dyed trinkets such as wooden cutouts, braid, feathers or star fish.

Materials

- *Dylon Multi-Purpose Dyes*: Golden Glow (02); Windsor Purple (15); Emerald (25); Kingfisher (33)
- *Dylon Cold Water Dyes*: Tahiti Rose (A11); Nasturtium (A18); Mexican Red (A21)
- methylated spirits (for *Dylon Cold Water Dyes*)
- balsa wood boxes with lids

Equipment

- sandpaper
- rubber gloves
- glass jug
- stirring utensil
- paint brushes
- spray sealer
- satin varnish

Materials

- *Dylon Multi-Purpose Dyes*: Golden Glow (02); Rose of Paris (12); Kingfisher (33)
- wooden toy box
- wooden clothes hook
- wooden table & chairs set

Equipment

- sandpaper
- rubber gloves
- glass jug
- stirring utensil
- paint brushes and sponges
- spray sealer
- satin varnish

Child's Room

These cheerful decorating ideas will liven up the play space. All of these items are created using only three colours.

Method for Table and Chairs Set and Wooden Toy Box

If possible disassemble wooden pieces so that you can paint sections separately. If it is not possible you will need to take extra care to ensure your dyes do not bleed from one area to another.

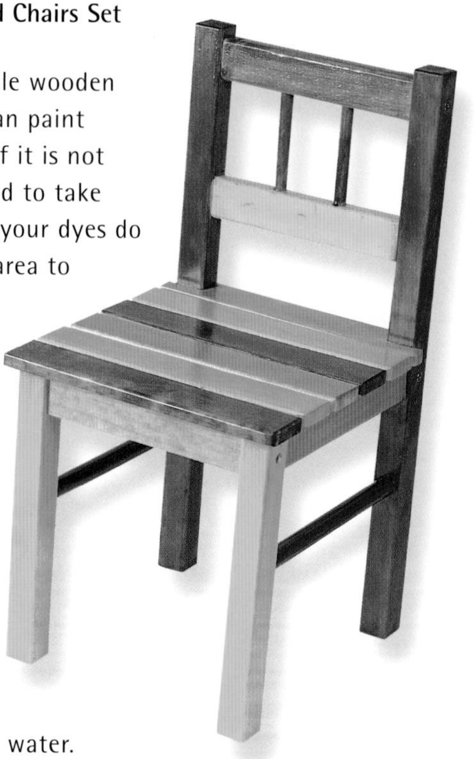

Rub down to bare wood and clean thoroughly. Ensure there is no varnish or other special finish remaining on the wood.

Wearing rubber gloves, pierce dye tin and dissolve the dye in 500mls of hot water.

Working on a protected surface, apply colour to wooden surface with a paint brush or sponge. With a slatted table and chairs such as the one shown here, brush on one colour on every third slat. Leave to dry before brushing on the next colour. Apply further coats to achieve required colour, allowing each coat to dry before applying the next one. Allow to dry before brushing dye on underneath surfaces.

Once thoroughly dry, apply a coat of spray sealer. Allow to dry and apply a coat of varnish. Lightly sand and apply varnish again.

It is a good idea to seal all underneath surfaces to prevent colours from running if they become wet.

Reassemble any objects which you took apart to dye. Dye matching fabric accessories as required.

Method for Clothes Hook

If possible disassemble hooks so you can paint sections separately. If it is not possible you will need to take extra care to ensure your dyes do not bleed from one area to another.

Rub down to bare wood and clean thoroughly. Ensure there is no varnish or other special finish remaining on the wood.

Wearing rubber gloves, pierce dye tin and dissolve the dye in 500mls of hot water.

Apply a coat of dye to the background area. Allow to dry. Apply further coats until you achieve the desired depth of colour.

Once thoroughly dry, apply a coat of spray sealer. Allow to dry and apply a coat of varnish. Lightly sand and apply another coat of varnish

With a brush, apply dye to the wood.

Tip
Varnish any surfaces which you do not want coloured before your start dyeing.

Materials
- *Dylon Multi-Purpose Dyes* and *Dylon Cold Water Dyes*: assorted colours
- methylated spirits (for *Dylon Cold Water Dyes*)
- wooden pegs

Equipment
- rubber gloves
- glass jug
- glass bowl
- stirring utensil
- tongs or sieve
- paper towel
- clear varnish

Decorative Pegs

These pretty pegs make wonderful message holders. Create a whole batch in red and green and use them to string Christmas cards throughout the house.

Method

Clean pegs and ensure there is no special finish on the wood. Wearing rubber gloves, pierce the dye tin and dissolve the dye according to instructions on page 12.

Pour solutions into glass bowls and add pegs, moving them around regularly with a stirring utensil to ensure an even colouring. Remove using metal tongs or a sieve and lay on paper towel to dry.

Follow this method for the wooden frames on pages 32–33. Apply a coat of clear varnish.

Glue a magnet to the back of the pegs and you create a handy memo holder for the fridge. Use the pegs to bundle recipes, letters and notes together or to hang this week's favourite drawing.

NOTE: DO NOT USE THE PEGS TO PEG OUT CLOTHES AS THE DYE MAY RUN.

Materials

- *Dylon Cold Water Dyes*: Nasturtium (A18);Mexican Red (A21);Bahama Blue (A23); Leaf Green (A24)
- methylated spirits
- wooden serviette rings
- wooden tray

Equipment

- sandpaper
- rubber gloves
- glass jug
- stirring utensil
- paper towel
- clear varnish

Serviette Rings and Tray

Liven up your dining table with some jazzy dyed bits and pieces in co-ordinating colours.

Method

Rub down the tray and rings to bare wood and clean thoroughly, ensuring there is no special finish remaining on the wood. Wearing rubber gloves pierce the dye tin and dissolve according to instructions on page 12 for dyeing wood with *Dylon Cold Water Dye.*

Working on a protected surface, brush the dye on the outside surfaces. Allow to dry on paper towel before brushing dye on the insides. Apply further coats to achieve the required colour.

Varnish the outside of each piece. Allow to dry then varnish the inside. Lightly sand and varnish again.

Tip

Wooden curtain rings make great serviette rings—just remove the

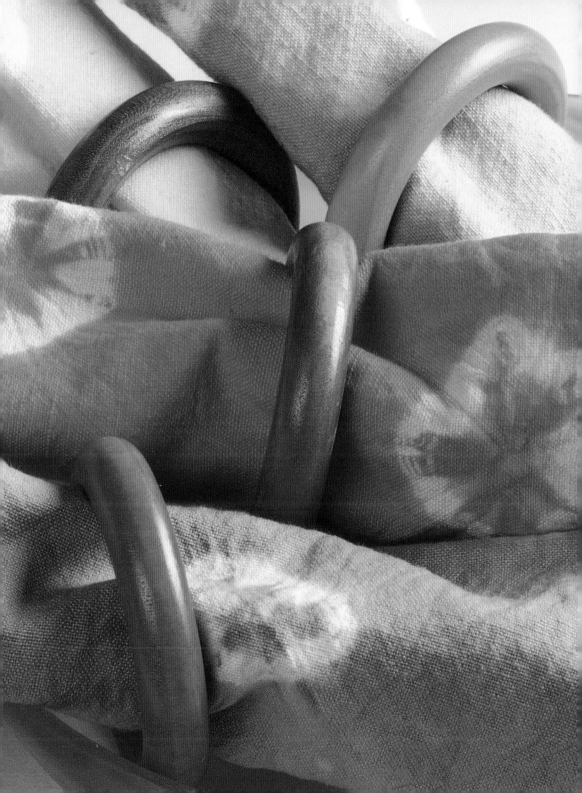

Interesting Ideas

Candles

Dyeing candles gives you this subtle, translucent look in the colours of your choice.

Method

Cut half a candle into small pieces and put into glass jug. Place the jug in saucepan of warm water. Heat until wax melts.

Add a little dye powder (approximately 1gm) to melted wax and stir well with metal spoon. You may need to experiment with the quantity of powder to achieve the required colour.

To the dyed wax, add 250mls of boiling water and stir. Keep this mixture over a low heat to prevent the wax from setting.

Dip the entire candle (holding it by the wick) into the solution. You must dip the candle and remove it quickly to prevent it from melting. Alternatively, you can create patterns by dipping the paint brush into the solution and dripping wax onto the candle.

The wax coating sets quickly and the decorated candles can be used within minutes of dyeing.

Materials

- *Dylon Cold Water Dyes*: Nasturtium (A18); Bahama Blue (A23); Leaf Green (A24)
- household candles

Equipment

- paint brushes
- saucepan
- glass jug
- metal spoon
- measuring spoon

Materials

- *Dylon Multi-Purpose Dyes*:
  Windsor Purple (15);
  Tangerine (39)
- wicker pieces

Equipment

- rubber gloves
- glass jug
- stirring utensil
- paint brushes

Wicker Pieces

Liven up natural wicker with bright contrasting colours to match your decor.

Method

This method works equally well for cane or other natural strands. Use smooth, unfinished wicker to ensure that the dye will be well absorbed. Make sure that the wicker is clean and dust-free.

Wearing rubber gloves, pierce dye tin and dissolve in 500mls of hot water. Working on a protected surface, brush on the dye to one side and leave the piece to dry. Turn the piece over and brush dye on the other side. Repeat until the piece is completely coloured to your taste. Apply further coats in the same way to achieve the required colour.

Use a clear varnish to protect dyed areas.

Papers and Feathers

Dyed papers and feathers make lovely personalised wrapping paper and decorations.

Method for Paper

Ensure paper is dust free. Wearing rubber gloves, pierce dye tin and and dissolve *Dylon Cold Water Dye* or *Dylon Multi-Purpose Dye* in 500mls of hot water. Using a sponge or paint brush dipped in the dye, apply colour to the paper. Apply evenly to achieve a uniform colour. For a mottled effect apply in patches. You could also flick dye for a splatter effect.

Dyed paper looks great as stationery. Use pale colours to dye paper when writing with ordinary inks and darker colours for stunning effects using metallic pens.

You can use the dyed paper in collages and scrap books and for making photograph mounts, cards, gift tags and even jewellery.

Method for Feathers

Dissolve the *Dylon Multi-Purpose Dye* in 500mls of boiling water. Fill dye bath with enough warm water to cover the feathers and add the dissolved dye. Add 500mls of vinegar.

Wash the feathers in soapy water, rinse thoroughly and add to dye bath soaking wet. Move feathers constantly for 10 minutes.

Remove the feathers from the solution and rinse until the water runs clear. Leave to dry. While the feathers are drying separate them carefully from one another to ensure they do not stick together.

Materials

- *Dylon Multi-Purpose Dyes* and *Dylon Cold Water Dyes*: assorted colours
- household vinegar (for feathers)
- handmade papers
- feathers

Equipment

- dye bath
- rubber gloves
- glass jug
- stirring utensil
- paint brushes or sponges

Apply the dye to the paper with a sponge or brush.

 Tip

Feathers are very fragile and should be handled with care throughout the entire process.

51

Materials

- *Dylon Multi-Purpose Dyes*:
  Golden Glow (2); Cherry
  Flame (10); Arabian Night (16)
- raffia

Equipment

- dye bath
- rubber gloves
- glass jug
- stirring utensil
- paper towel

Raffia

*Dye raffia in every colour of the rainbow
and use it to make attractive table
decorations or to add colour and interest
to a hat.*

Method

Dissolve the dye in 500mls of boiling water. Fill the
dye bath with very hot water and add the dissolved
dye.

   Wet the raffia completely and then submerge in the
dye bath. Gently move the raffia around the dye bath
to make sure that all areas are covered.

   Remove the raffia from the solution once the
required colour is achieved. Rinse carefully and allow
to dry by laying it on paper towel.

   During the drying process tap the strands gently to
ensure they do not stick together.

Tip
The shades obtained on
raffia are not as intense
as on dyed fabric.

52

Tassels

Use dyeing to create co-ordinating tassels and tassel heads to add a stylish flourish to your furnishings.

Method

The different materials used will mean that your tassel shows several shades of the same colour on the various parts.

Wearing rubber gloves, pierce the dye tin and dissolve in 500mls of warm water in glass jug. Add *Dylon Cold Dye Fix* dissolved in hot water with 125gms salt. Roll the fringes and hold in place with pins. Submerge the rolled fringes, gimp braid, cord, decorative lace, and the wooden tassel head in the dye. Soak in dye for approximately one hour. Remove and allow to dry.

When the wooden tassel head is dry, finish off with several coats of varnish. For variety the wooden tassel could be painted or gilded.

Assemble the tassel as follows: apply craft glue to the lower end of the tassel head. Wrap the wider fringe around the glue and apply more glue and continue winding and gluing the fringe to the tassel head. Allow to dry slightly. Continue gluing and winding, this time using the narrow fringe. Then glue the lace around the top edge of the fringe. Glue the gimp braid on top to cover all edges. Fold the cord in half and glue the ends into the top of the tassel head.

Steam the completed tassel over a boiling kettle to restore the fringes to a tangle-free state.

Tip

Ensure the type of fringing, braid, cord and lace is correct fibre type for dyeing. See chart page 13 for more details.

Materials

- *Dylon Cold Water Dyes*: Purple Vine (A19): Sahara Sun (A22); Bahama Blue (A23)
- *Dylon Cold Dye Fix*
- salt
- wooden tassel head
- 35cm of 150mm wide fringe
- 35cm of 75mm wide fringe
- 15cm gimp braid
- 30cm cord
- 15cm decorative lace

Equipment

- rubber gloves
- glass jug
- stirring utensil
- paint brush
- paper towel
- satin varnish
- pins
- craft glue
- scissors

Submerge the rolled fringe into the dye.

Materials
- *Dylon Multi-Purpose Dyes* and *Dylon Cold Water Dyes*: assorted colours
- lima beans & chick peas

Equipment
- dye bath
- rubber gloves
- glass bowl
- stirring utensil
- metal sieve
- paper towel
- decorative bottles

Grains and Beans

Dyed grains and beans make unusual and effective decorations for your kitchen.

Method
Wash the beans lightly to remove any debris. Do not leave them to soak as they will swell and change shape.

Wearing rubber gloves, pierce the dye tin and dissolve dye in 250mls of warm water. Pour into a glass bowl large enough to dip your sieve into. Pour the beans into the sieve and dip into the dye bath and lift out repeatedly until you have the desired colour. Do not leave them to soak. Spread beans on paper towel to dry.

When you have a variety of shapes and colours prepared, layer them in decorative clear glass bottles and cut a piece of cork to use as a stopper. You could attach a piece of dyed raffia (see page 52) around the neck of the jars to decorate them.

Submerge the sieve in the dye.

Flowers
and Grasses

*Dried flowers or grasses can make
an attractive feature in any room.*

Method

Wearing rubber gloves, pierce the dye tin and dissolve
the dye in 500mls of hot water. Fill the dye bath with
very hot water and add the dissolved dye.

Wet the dried flowers or grasses completely and
then submerge in the dye bath. Gently move them
around the dye bath to make sure that all areas are
covered.

Remove the dried flowers or grasses from the
solution once the desired colour is achieved. Rinse
carefully and allow to dry by laying it on paper towel.

During the drying process tap the dried flowers or
grasses gently to separate.

Materials

- *Dylon Multi-Purpose Dyes*:
  Carnival (13); Windsor Purple
  (15); Emerald (25); Kingfisher
  (33); Tangerine (39)
- dried flowers or grasses

Equipment

- dye bath
- rubber gloves
- glass jug
- stirring utensil
- paper towel

 Tip

The quantity of dye needed
depends on the depth of
colour required. The shades
obtained will not be as
intense as those achieved
on dyed fabric.

Antique Tea Dyeing

Create an attractive and colourfast antique effect using this mock tea-dye method.

Materials
- *Dylon Cold Water Dye*: Koala Brown (A29)
- *Dylon Cold Dye Fix*
- salt
- fabric toy

Equipment
- dye bath
- rubber gloves
- glass jug
- stirring utensil

Method

Wearing rubber gloves, pierce the dye tin and dissolve dye in 500mls of very hot tap water.

Fill the dye bath with enough cold water to allow the fabric toy to move freely.

Varied shades can be achieved by adding greater or lesser amounts of the dissolved dye to the dye bath. For a pale colour add 25mls; for a light colour add 50mls; for a medium colour add 100mls; for a dark colour add 200mls. Add the desired amount of dye mixture.

Dissolve 125gms of salt and *Dylon Cold Dye Fix* in very hot tap water and add to the dye bath.

Plunge the clean, damp fabric toy into the dye bath and agitate for the first 10 minutes and at intervals during the next 50 minutes.

Allow the water to drain away from the dye bath. Squeeze the liquid from the toy and rinse it in cold water until the water runs clear. Hot wash it and hang it to dry. When drying, peg parts of the toy which will be covered by clothing in order to avoid marking the exposed fabric.

Pale

Light

Medium

Dark

Dylon Advice Line

For further information on Dylon products or on dyeing, contact the Dylon Advice Line on 020 8663 4296.

Acknowledgements

The Publisher gratefully acknowledges the people and organisations (listed here in alphabetical order) who contributed items for this book:

Dinosaur Designs

Dulux Paints

Grada's Garden Florist

Ikea

Laura Ashley

Porters Paints

Quilt designed and made by Kate McEwen

Scripted Fabric designed and made by Kellie Steedman

Scripted Cushion made by Kate McEwen

Week 9

C O L L I N S

GERMAN SHEPHERD DOG

AN OWNER'S GUIDE

The authors

Dr Peter Neville DHc BSc (Hons) is
a Director of the Centre of Applied Pet
Ethology (COAPE) group of practices,
research and educational services. He
has been in practice for the treatment
of pet behaviour problems for over
ten years. A frequent lecturer and
broadcaster on pet behaviour, he is
also the author of some internationally
best-selling books.

Hazel Palmer MAPBC divides her time
between working at the University of
East London and professional pet
behaviour counselling. She runs the
pioneering Stratford Pet Dog Club.

Sarah Whitehead BA (Hons) is a full-
time pet behaviour counsellor and a
leading figure in the establishment of
puppy classes and modern reward-based
dog training.

David Cavill has been breeding,
exhibiting, judging, photographing
and writing about dogs for over twenty
five years. He is the publisher of Dogs
Monthly and Our Dogs and Cats in the
UK. His courses on showing, judging,
breeding and animal care, which were
written for the Animal Care College,
are taken up by hundreds of students.

Veterinary authors

John Bower BVSc, MRCVS is a senior
partner in a small animal Veterinary
Hospital in Plymouth, England. He
has served as President of both the
British Veterinary Association and
the British Small Animal Veterinary
Association. He writes regularly for
the veterinary press and also for dog
and cat publications. He is co-author
of two dog healthcare books and a
member of the Kennel Club.

Caroline Bower BVMS, MRCVS
runs a veterinary health centre in
the same practice as John. Her special
interests include prevention and
treatment of behavioural problems,
and she lectures to dog breeding and
training groups.

COLLINS

GERMAN SHEPHERD DOG

AN OWNER'S GUIDE

Dr Peter Neville and Associates

HarperCollins*Publishers*

First published in 1996 by
HarperCollins*Publishers*
London

© HarperCollins*Publishers* Ltd 1996
© Photographs: François Nicaise and HarperCollins*Publishers* Ltd 1996

Peter Neville asserts the moral right to be identified as the author of this work.

A catalogue record of this book is available
from the British Library

ISBN 0 00 412903 2

This book was created by SP Creative Design for HarperCollins*Publishers* Ltd
Editor: Heather Thomas
Designers: Al Rockall and Rolando Ugolini
Production: Diane Clouting

Photography:
François Nicaise: Cover and pages 1, 6-7, 9, 10, 11, 12, 16, 17, 19, 20, 23, 24, 26, 27, 29, 31, 32, 34, 40, 52-53, 55, 56, 57, 58, 59, 61, 64, 69, 77, 78, 79, 82, 85, 86, 89, 90, 92, 94-95
David Dalton: Back cover and pages 3, 14-15, 36, 38, 41, 43, 45, 46, 47, 48, 49, 50, 51, 62, 63, 67, 68, 70, 71, 73, 75, 80, 81, 83, 84
Frank Lane Picture Library: page 25

Acknowledgements
The Breed Standard used by kind permission of the Kennel Club.
The publishers would like to thank the following for their kind assistance in producing this book:
Scampers School for Dogs for their help with photography, and special thanks to Charlie Clarricoates for all his hard work
Mary Cresswell and her German Shepherd Dogs, Scotfame Firecracker, Scotfame Katrine and Scotfame Queen of the Meadow

Colour reproduction by Colourscan, Singapore
Printed and bound by New Interlitho SpA, Italy

CONTENTS

PART ONE

YOU AND YOUR DOG

German Shepherd Dogs are probably the most popular breed of dog in the world today. This is largely due to their versatility and the characteristics that make them outstanding companions as well as excellent working dogs in a range of widely varying situations. Although they are used as police and service dogs, drug detection dogs, search and rescue dogs, guide dogs and disabled support dogs, the majority of German Shepherds are family pets. Alert, responsive and loyal, they are highly trainable, whether their role is as a working partner or as a companion dog.

Originally a herding dog in rural Germany, the German Shepherd's appearance and behaviour are determined to a great extent by its earlier working role. Many owners find that their dogs tend to 'herd' them when they are out walking in the park or countryside.

CHAPTER ONE

HISTORY OF THE GERMAN SHEPHERD DOG

BREED ORIGINS

The German Shepherd Dog evolved in Germany in the late nineteenth century and its emergence as a breed was due to the far-sighted vision of one man, a cavalry officer called Max von Stephanitz.

At that time, many working sheep-dogs were used by the farmers living throughout the rural areas of Germany. Although they varied in appearance, there were two main types of dogs that were of particular importance to the later development of the German Shepherd Dog as a breed.

The sheepdogs working in highland Thuringia were generally wolf-grey in colour with erect ears, both desirable qualities, but they were small and stocky and often had curled tails. However, the dogs from Wurttemberg were generally larger and heavier boned, with a bushy tail. These dogs were swift and had a good gait but poor ear carriage.

The first occasion on which dogs of both these types were exhibited in a show was in Hanover in 1882, and ten years later, in 1892, the Phylax Society was

formed. Although this was not successful, it was the inspiration for the formation of the *Verein für Deutsche Schaferhunde*, or SV, which was initiated on 22nd April 1899. The first president was Adolf Meyer, followed in 1901 by Max von Stephanitz.

A breed standard was drawn up and the SV held its first breed show, or *Sieger*, in September 1899, and the titles of *Sieger* and *Siegerin* were awarded to the top male and female dogs respectively.

So there was now a breed club for the various types of sheepdogs working in Germany, and dogs could be registered. The first dog registered was of great significance to the breed; he was widely used at stud and was, to a great extent, the model on which the breed was based. He was a Thuringian-type dog called Horand v Grafrath SZ 1 (formerly Hektor Linksrhein) and was owned by Max von Stephanitz himself.

The German Shepherd Dog is powerful, agile and well-muscled.

Horand's most famous offspring was Hector v Schwaben who won the title *Sieger* (equivalent to Grand Champion) in both 1900 and 1901. Hector's dam, a Wurttemberg-type herding bitch called Mores Plieningen, was also a major influence on the breed.

The SV was controlled extremely effectively by von Stephanitz, and soon the membership and the numbers of dogs registered grew rapidly – there were thirty-one members of the SV in 1899, increasing to 3,500 by 1912. This growth has continued to the present day with the SV now being the largest breed society in the world.

Hector sired 141 progeny, and of these the three most important were his sons Heinz v Starkenberg and the litter brothers Beowulf and Pilot. Heinz sired the all black dog Roland v Starkenberg which was widely used at stud, won *Sieger* titles in both Austria and Germany and is recognised as being a major influence on the breed's future. Other significant dogs of that time were Horst v Boll and the bitch Flora (Berkemeyer).

The German Shepherd Dog became firmly established in Germany and soon it became popular in other countries of Europe and overseas. In 1906 the first dog was exported to the United States.

Laios van Noort, the UK Champion German Shepherd Dog, is owned by Wendy and Graham Stephens.

Indiscriminate breeding was a problem even in those early years, and there was concern about the increasing physical size of the dog and problems with temperament. With this in mind, von Stephanitz established the first breed surveyors in 1921 so that dogs could be assessed both physically and mentally. The various forms of assessment used continue to this day in Germany where a German Shepherd Dog has to demonstrate not only its ability to work but also to protect its owner. Dogs are required also to gain a working qualification (*Schutzhund*) before they can be passed

for breeding. A competition is held every year in Germany at which the competing dogs are assessed for their ability to herd sheep as they did in those early years of their development.

All white German Shepherd Dogs are growing in popularity, but they are not recognised by purists and they may sometimes have behaviour problems.

THE BREED STANDARD

The distinctive character and versatility of the German Shepherd have come from von Stephanitz's vision of the breed as a working dog. His original role was as a herding dog and as such he required the correct physical construction to trot for long periods. From this a standard was laid down for the breed, which is used as a blueprint for the ideal dog. It is this breed standard that a judge relates to when he assesses dogs in a show ring, and it is also what breeders refer to when deciding on which dogs to use in a breeding programme, to enable the qualities of one dog to complement another. It takes a great deal of experience to be able to look at a dog and his pedigree and to decide whether the use of a particular dog will enhance the qualities that the breeder already has in his dog's line.

The Breed Standard

(used by kind permission of the Kennel Club)

General Appearance

Slightly long in comparison to height; of powerful, well-muscled build with a weather-resistant coat. Relation between height, length, position and structure of

The German Shepherd Dog should always conform to the breed standard.

fore and hindquarters (angulation) producing far-reaching, enduring gait. Clear definition of masculinity and femininity is essential, and working ability never sacrificed for mere beauty.

Characteristics

A versatile working dog, balanced and free from exaggeration. Attentive, alert, resilient and tireless with a keen scenting ability.

Temperament

Steady of nerve, loyal, self-assured, courageous and tractable. Never nervous, over-aggressive or shy.

Head and skull

Proportionate in size to body, never coarse, too fine or long. Clean cut; fairly broad between ears. Forehead slightly domed; little or no trace of central furrow. Cheeks forming softly rounded curve, never protruding. Skull from ears to bridge of nose tapering gradually and evenly, blending without too pronounced stop into wedge-shaped powerful muzzle. Skull approximately 50 per cent of overall length of head. Width of skull corresponding approximately to length, in males slightly greater, in females slightly less. Muzzle strong, lips firm, clean and closing tightly. Top of muzzle straight, almost parallel to forehead. Short, blunt, weak, pointed, overlong muzzle undesirable.

continued overleaf

THE BREED STANDARD

Used by kind permission of the Kennel Club

Eyes
Medium-sized, almond-shaped, never protruding. Dark brown preferred, lighter shade permissible, provided expression good and general harmony of head not destroyed. Expression lively, intelligent and self-assured.

Ears
Medium-sized, firm in texture, broad at base, set high, carried erect, almost parallel, never pulled inwards or tipped, tapering to a point, open at front. Never hanging. Folding back during movement permissible.

Mouth
Jaws strongly developed. With a perfect, regular and complete scissor bite, i.e. upper teeth closely over-lapping lower teeth and set square to the jaws. Teeth healthy and strong. Full dentition desirable.

Neck
Fairly long, strong with well developed muscles, free from throatiness. Carried at 45 degrees angle to horizontal, raised when excited, lowered at fast trot.

Forequarters
Shoulder blades long, set obliquely (45 degrees) laid flat to body. Upper arm strong, well muscled, joining shoulder blade at approximately 90 degrees. Forelegs straight from pasterns to elbows viewed from any angle, bone oval rather than round. Pasterns firm, supple and slightly angulated. Elbows neither tucked in nor turned out. Length of foreleg exceeding depth of chest.

SIZE

Ideal height (from withers and just touching elbows): dogs 62.5 cms (25 ins) bitches 57.5 cms (23 ins). 2.5 cms (1 in) either above or below ideal permissible.

Body

Length measured from point of breast bone to rear edge of pelvis, exceeding height at the withers. Correct ratio 10 to 9 or 8 and a half. Under-sized dogs, stunted growth, high-legged dogs, those too heavy or too light in build, overloaded fronts, too short overall appearance, any feature detracting from reach or endurance of gait, undesirable. Chest deep (45-48 per cent) of height at shoulder, not too broad, brisket long, well developed. Ribs well formed and long, neither barrel-shaped nor too flat; allowing free movement of elbows when gaiting.

Relatively short loin. Belly firm, only slightly drawn up. Back between withers and croup, straight, strongly developed, not too long. Overall length achieved by correct angle of well-laid shoulders, correct length of croup and hindquarters. Withers long, of good height and well defined, joining back in a smooth line without disrupting flowing topline, slightly sloping from front to back. Weak, soft and roach backs undesirable and should be rejected. Loin broad, strong, well muscled. Croup long, gently curving downwards to tail without disrupting flowing topline. Short, steep or flat croups undesirable.

Hindquarters

Overall strong, broad and well muscled, enabling effortless forward propulsion of whole body. Upper thighbone, viewed from side, sloping to slightly longer lower thighbone. Hind angulation sufficient if imaginary line dropped from point of buttocks cuts through lower thigh just in front of hock, continuing down slightly in front of hind feet. Angulations corresponding with front angulation, without over-angulation, hock strong. Any tendency towards over-angulation of hindquarters reduces firmness and endurance.

Feet

Rounded toes well closed and arched. Pads well cushioned and durable. Nails short, strong and dark in colour. Dew claws removed from hindlegs.

Tail

Bushy-haired, reaches at least to hock – ideal length reaching to middle of metatarsus. At rest tail hangs in slight sabre-like curve; when moving raised and curve increased, ideally never above level of back. Short, rolled, curled, generally carried badly or stumpy from birth, undesirable.

THE BREED STANDARD (CONTINUED)

Gait/Movement Sequence of step follows diagonal pattern, moving foreleg and opposite hindleg forward simultaneously; hindfoot thrust forward to midpoint of body and having equally long reach with forefeet without any noticeable change in backline.

Coat Outer coat consisting of straight, hard, close-lying hair as dense as possible; thick undercoat. Hair on head, ears, front of legs, paws and toes short; on back,longer and thicker; in some males forming slight ruff. Hair longer on back of legs as far down as pasterns and stifles forming fairly thick trousers on hindquarters. No hard and fast rule for length of hair; mole-type coats undesirable.

Colour Black or black saddle with tan, or gold to light grey markings. All black, all grey, with lighter or brown markings referred to as Sables. Nose black. Light markings on chest or very pale colour on inside of legs permissible but undesirable, as are whitish nails, red-tipped tails or wishy-washy faded colours defined as lacking in pigmentation. Blues, livers, albinos, whites (i.e. almost pure white dogs with black noses) and near whites *highly undesirable*. Undercoat, except in all black dogs, usually grey or fawn. Colour in itself is of secondary importance having no effect on character or fitness for work. Final colour of a young dog only ascertained when outer coat has developed.

Faults Any departure from the foregoing points should be considered a fault and the seriousness with which the fault should be regarded should be in exact proportion to its degree.

Note Male animals should have two apparently normal testicles fully descended into the scrotum.

THE GERMAN SHEPHERD DOG AT WORK

Police dogs

The German Shepherd is the breed most widely used for police work and security duties throughout the world. This is due to his effectiveness as a versatile and courageous protection dog. When performing a job of work, the German Shepherd is a most outstanding animal. No other dog has been found as suitable to carry out a wide range of tasks, although some other breeds, such as Dobermans, Rottweilers, Weimeraners and Bouviers des Flandres, have also been used as police dogs.

Some police forces breed their own dogs, whereas others accept dogs as gifts from the general public. These dogs are accepted for a short stay while they are tested for physical health, and assessed for temperament and suitability for training. If accepted, they are allocated to a handler and are required to complete a lengthy training course. The dogs that pass become working police dogs.

As such, they are required to carry out a range of tasks with their handlers. Adaptability and temperament are of the utmost importance in a dog, which may need to face a criminal with a gun in the morning, be on crowd control duty at a football match in the afternoon, and search for a lost child in the evening.

New or prospective owners wishing to see the German Shepherd Dog in its working role can visit police dog championships and displays, which are held regularly in several countries, including Great Britain.

These competitions are designed to test dogs in a wide range of exercises and situations, any of which could occur in the working police dog's daily routine. The dogs are required to track and follow a scent which will be many hours old, and to find articles along the track and indicate their position to their handlers.

In addition, they are expected to carry out a range of obedience exercises, e.g. walking to heel, staying etc., and to demonstrate their agility by jumping a high upright scale jump, as well as a long jump. They are also required to search an area for a person who is hidden, and to indicate their presence to the handler, and to challenge and stop an armed man. The German Shepherd's retrieving ability is also tested on objects as diverse as metal pipes and buckets.

Service dogs

German Shepherd Dogs are used in many roles with the armed services of various countries, patrolling defence establishments. Some dogs are trained specifically

As police dogs, German Shepherds are trained to perform a wide range of tasks. They have to be tested for agility, obedience and skill.

to sniff out weapons and explosives, which may be buried underground or hidden in a vehicle.

Drug detection dogs

German Shepherd Dogs are also used to seek out prohibited drugs which may be smuggled through airports and ports. The 'sniffer dogs' undergo a rigorous training programme to test them in a range of different situations, from noisy engine rooms of ships to aircraft hangars and warehouses piled high with parcels.

This dog is assisting his handler in searching a vehicle for hidden drugs.

The dog's sense of smell is so acute that he is able to pick up minute traces of the scent of drugs, such as cannabis, heroin, amphetamines etc. A dog is very efficient in this role as he can cover a wide area very quickly and will indicate the presence of any of these drugs to his handler. Drugs are often hidden in cars and container lorries as well as in parcels, and the dog has become a major force in fighting drug smuggling across the world, even to the extent where drug smuggling gangs in the United States have put out 'contracts' to kill dogs which have found millions of dollars' worth of drugs.

Guide dogs

German Shepherd Dogs were one of the first breeds used as guides for blind owners when the Seeing Eye programme was set up in the United States. Although Labradors and Labrador crosses are now the most popular breeds used, German Shepherds still make up approximately one-third of the guide dogs working with their blind owners in Great Britain. German Shepherd Dogs are selected frequently for owners who lead very busy lives and where the dog is required to be on duty for many hours each day.

Disabled and support dogs

This is a new but rapidly growing area in which dogs are used to assist their disabled owners in a variety of ways in normal everyday life. Dogs are specially trained and allocated to particular owners or, alternatively, the pets of disabled owners can be retrained. The German Shepherds working in these schemes have been trained by the use of rewards to carry out a range of tasks, including bringing the phone to the owner, picking up named articles, acting as a support to help the owner to move

SEARCH AND RESCUE DOGS

German Shepherds are used in many countries as search and rescue dogs. They may spend many hours with their handlers in atrocious conditions on mountainsides searching for climbers who have become lost or may have been injured. These dogs are winched down by helicopter and can cover large areas much more quickly and efficiently than a man on his own. They are also used after earthquakes and explosions to search amongst the rubble of the demolished buildings for people who have been buried.

position, removing washing from the machine and even collecting goods from shops while their owners wait outside.

PAT dogs

Pro Dogs Active Therapy, or PAT Dogs, are pets of calm, steady temperament which are taken by their owners into hospitals and old people's homes etc. Many German Shepherds are registered to perform these visits.

Companion dogs

The vast majority of German Shepherds, however, are family pets, and their reputation as an all-round companion has led to their deserved position as one of the most popular breeds of dog registered by Kennel Clubs throughout the world.

BEHAVIOUR & TRAINING

EVOLUTION OF THE DOG

There is no question that the alert, responsive German Shepherd Dog, be he long – or short-coated, black, black and tan, grey or white, rightfully deserves his place in our hearts as one of our favourite breeds of dog. But how has he come about? Why does the unquestionably loyal, highly trainable German Shepherd Dog behave differently to the ancestor of all dogs, the wolf, even when he looks so similar, and why does he make such a marvellous pet for the modern family when he was developed originally as a working stock herding dog? We will try to answer some of these questions in this chapter.

Behaviour and appearance

The man/dog relationship has existed since prehistoric times; it began in the Mesolithic period, about 10,000 to 14,000 years ago, and then progressed with little change until this century. In the past, man predominantly bred German Shepherd Dogs, and indeed all other dogs, for what they did and the roles they performed and not for how they looked. However, in the last hundred years or so, there has been a shift of emphasis away

from the selection of a dog's ability to perform particular tasks to one based on a dog's appearance and also its social temperament.

This has been caused mainly by the massive rise in ownership of dogs kept purely as pets with little or no obligation to work or contribute to the family pack other than as companions. In the past fifty years or so (0.005 per cent of the time that man has had a relationship with the dog), our expectations of what dogs should look like and how they should behave have altered enormously.

This shift in emphasis probably lies at the root of many of the physical and behavioural problems now seen in some of our modern breeds of dog. However, the adaptable and intelligent German Shepherd Dog seems to have made the change from his main role as working partner and herding dog to that of family pet and companion with far fewer problems than many other breeds of dog.

German Shepherd Dogs are remarkably similar in appearance to their ancestor, the wolf, from whom all today's breeds of dog have evolved.

SURVIVAL IN A CHANGING ENVIRONMENT

The three survival imperatives for any animal are feeding, reproducing and staying out of trouble. Physical changes in an animal are triggered by changes in the environment, and its behavioural adaptations to ensure its survival. The change in the environment that facilitated the domestication of the wolf into the dog occurred when man began to adopt a village way of life. This provided the possibility of a year-round stable food supply for wild animals if they could

move in near enough to him to exploit it.

The rubbish dumps just outside man's villages and settlements would have been a good source of food for scavenging wolves and other animals. They would also have provided a safe place for juvenile wolves to be left by the adults when they went on hunting excursions.

The juvenile wolves that benefited most from the stable food supply and security of these dumps were those that learned to live and survive close to man

Wolves live and hunt in packs, each with its own highly organised social structure, pack 'rules' and communications system.

without running away, and the more confident ones would soon have become able to enter the village to scavenge.

Man's switch from a hunter/gatherer lifestyle to being mainly a crop farmer would have made an easily obtainable year-round meat supply highly advantageous. Juicy young wolves would fit on the menu nicely and so it would have suited man to tolerate their scavenging activities. Once a resident population of young wolves was established in the village and had stayed to reach maturity and breed there, man would soon have become aware of which wolf/dogs produced the biggest and fattest puppies and encouraged them for eating later. Direct physical contact and socialization of village-born puppies with man would then have occurred as a crucial part of the taming and domestication process.

Early village dogs

These would have been indirectly encouraged by man to grow up retaining the playful characteristics of juvenile wolves and not to develop the fully dominant or predatory behaviours that are typical of adult wolves. In this way, man could accept them without danger to himself. These characteristics became established in the adult reproductive population of village dogs.

■ **Hunting dogs** Some dogs would have retained near-adult qualities in terms of their predatory behaviour patterns and would have been ideal for helping man to stalk his prey when he went out to hunt.

■ **Herding dogs** These dogs could also have proved useful in helping man to herd his sheep and other livestock outside the village.

■ **Guarding dogs** Village dogs that remained very juvenile in their behaviour and showed no propensity either for hunting or herding would have been ideal for guarding man's livestock.

■ **Retrieving dogs** Other slightly more adult types would have developed strong possessive instincts over objects and these would have been selected by man to train to use as retrievers on the hunt.

Thus herding, stalking, heeling, retrieving and guarding types of dog would all have evolved from less socially competitive, less predatory animals, and each of these types of dog seems to arise from a distinct arrested stage of development of the wolf.

Dogs that performed well at what they were expected to do would have been kept and bred from, and their skills refined in most cases through specific types of training, while others that were

German Shepherd Dogs were bred originally as herding dogs in the rural sheep-farming areas of Germany.

BREEDING FOR BEHAVIOUR

The popularity of the dog occurred initially because it was viewed as a year-round source of food in man's early villages. Certainly most modern races of man developed from early dog-eating peoples and approximately sixty per cent of the human race still has a cultural attachment to eating dog meat to some degree. Later the dog was prized as a hunter/guard working companion, and slowly started to be transported by man around the world via the trade routes to places where he had not evolved through the village process. As working animals, dogs would have been much valued, but the dog type that excelled at herding in one settlement may have looked entirely different to the one that had evolved to do the same job in another. Much like the gamekeeper, farmer or sporting huntsman of today, if the dog was good at his job, it didn't matter how he looked. Selection for breeding was based on a dog's behaviour in terms of doing the job he was intended for, and this is what established the appearance of his type and his physical ability to do the job required.

not so good would probably have been driven out or even killed and eaten. At this stage, and for the subsequent. thousands of years, man did not care what his dog looked like; he was only interested in what it did. Dogs were solely bred for their behavioural characteristics and it was man's selection for these attributes that encouraged the different types of dog to evolve.

BEHAVIOUR VERSUS TEMPERAMENT

Many dogs (including the German Shepherd Dog) were originally bred to perform tasks far removed from the largely indoor lives they now lead. Paradoxically, of course, if behavioural changes in dog types are so inherently and originally linked to physical changes, selecting primarily for their appearance, as practised in the show world, must inevitably destabilize the predictability of this behaviour. We should not be surprised that so many dogs develop behaviour problems when bred and required mainly for their looks rather than selecting for the ability to do the job that originally made them the way they look. Nor should we be surprised that there are now so many canine psychologists to help them to cope with their new lifestyles.

Measuring temperament

We interpret 'behaviour' as expressing what a dog has been physically and genetically programmed to do, whilst 'temperament' is considered to be an emotional response which dictates how it utilizes these programmed skills. 'Good temperament' in a pet dog usually means that it is friendly with other dogs and people, especially children. Therefore temperament is measured more by considerations of its sociability rather than by its working behaviour.

Hunting and gathering

The German Shepherd is a herder type of dog. His predatory sequence has become truncated to 'detect/eye/ follow/stalk/ chase' through deliberate selection of dogs that did not complete the final stages of 'grasp/bite /kill' in the hunting sequence. He is interruptible at any stage of this sequence, readily trainable on signals to divert his attention to us.

GUARDING DOGS

Subsequent and more recent selection for tasks other than herding, such as guarding, arises from the German Shepherd's high level of sensitivity and reactivity at the 'detect/eye' stage of the predatory sequence. His worldwide use as a general patrol dog for the police and armed forces arises from his excellent senses of hearing, scent and eyesight, and emotional reactivity with the interruptible predatory sequence of the herder. This makes him easy to train once you have learned to signal correctly and without force, including when needing to direct his renowned willingness to learn to display controlled aggressive behaviour.

THE GERMAN SHEPHERD IN THE HUMAN PACK

The attributes needed for a good herding dog are not only a reliable, controllable sequence of predatory behaviour as far as we need it to go, but also a willingness to accept our interruption of that behaviour. By necessity, the herding dog's predatory instincts demand a high level of sensitivity to sound, scent and movement. Couple this with our demand for any dog to be socially appeasing and directible, and herding types, such as the German Shepherd Dog, quickly became useful to us for performing a wide range of other tasks.

The German Shepherd was good at the original tasks of herding cattle and sheep, and later at guarding and scent following. He has always enjoyed long years of working partnership with his owner/handler, and it is no surprise that he is bred to pass on these attributes.

However, it seems that selection based on performance causes certain physical attributes to be maintained in the herder type, most notably muscular strength, stamina and agility. These features are probably less likely to be maintained when selecting for other broader behavioural characteristics in the breeding of a more general-purpose working type, especially when the breed is more likely to be selected primarily for the degree to which it conforms to the

changing fads of the human view of ideal
appearance in the dog show ring. As a
result, smaller, slimmer and less robust
looking dogs soon arose and now predomi-
nate, notably with sloping (roach) backs,
and with less predictable but nonetheless
reactive and sensitive behaviour patterns
then those of their working forebears.

Adaptability

Clearly today, an understanding of a particular breed's original working type
should be a main priority for the owner of
any dog, as well as for the dog trainer or
canine behaviourist. In the process of
selecting for working type in our dogs, we
have deliberately excluded dogs that, in a
social conflict, showed a tendency to
select 'fight' as their coping strategy (see
box). Later, we found such qualities desirable for certain tasks in some types and so
selected dogs that would adopt 'fight' as
their coping strategy, but now with a more
controllable edge as a result of their

THE FOUR 'F' STRATEGIES

- Fight ■ Flight
- Freeze ■ Fiddle about

Aggression is one of the four strategies
for coping with the fear of threats and
challenges – it is the 'fight' response,
with 'flight (running away)', 'freeze (and
hope to go unnoticed)' and 'fiddle about'
(appease) being the other alternatives.

TRAINABILITY

The German Shepherd is easy to train:
- Its sensitivity and reactivity as a
herder.
- Its willingness to be socially appeasing
('fiddle about') to resolve conflicts with
members of its own social group.
- Its willingness to adopt 'threaten to
fight' or 'fight' tactics against outside
threats.

domesticated willingness to be socially
appeasing. These types of dog would have
been the forerunners of today's guarding
breeds, such as the German Shepherd,
where the 'fight' strategy is harnessed and
directed at challenges outside the dog's
immediate pack.

If a sensitive, intelligent herding
type of dog, such as the German
Shepherd Dog, is not worked as a herder,
nor directed and trained to other jobs
that it can perform, it is far more likely
than possibly any other type of dog to
become very reactive in any circumstances, either social or 'predatory', and
become unstable in the human home
and family. On the other hand, if we are
prepared to school the temperament of
German Shepherds, manage their
sensitivity, apply their outstanding
intelligence, the skills of their type and
exercise their remarkable ability to
communicate with us, they are
very rewarding pet dogs to own.

HOW DOGS COMMUNICATE — WHAT IS LANGUAGE?

The development of language has arisen out of the need for some animals to communicate with each other in order to survive, both in finding a mate and, in animals such as wolves, in developing the necessary co-operative social skills in order to hunt, and protect shared resources of food, shelter and breeding areas together. Expressing emotions, direction and intention by one animal and their interpretation by another and subsequent organization of responses enables each to predict the behaviour of the other and so contribute to their combined success.

In most social mammals, such communication takes three major forms of direct language:

- Vocal signals
- Body/facial movements
- Touch

Dogs largely learn the direct language skills demanded for a social lifestyle between the ages of weaning and puberty, schooled under the protective supervision of their parents and other older members of the group into which they are destined to integrate. The position of the ears, the degree of opening of the eyes and direction of stare, and the opening of the mouth and display of teeth are all used to help signal anxiety, excitement, fear or invitation to approach and play, and help communicate an enormous range of moods expressed by dogs, one to another.

Communicating mood

When signalling an assertive mood or intent in a social encounter, the wolf or dog stands upright with his tail usually held high and perhaps arched over his back, his head held up and ears erect to convey a message of being large and powerful. A wolf signalling subordination

The expressive German Shepherd Dog communicates with his eyes and ears.

A dog that is signalling submission to a packmate may roll on to its back.

in such an encounter, on the other hand, may drop its body and keep its head below the level of its back with its ears flattened. Additionally, a submissive dog may also withdraw its lips and 'grin' as it approaches a higher ranking packmate, often in association with other signs of submission. A dramatic and perhaps last-resort communication of passive submission is shown when a dog rolls on its back and presents its underbelly.

Communication via scent

Many animals, including dogs, may also communicate using the indirect language of visual marks and pheromones – chemical messengers of scent. Scent marking enables signals to remain in the environment for longer periods than direct forms of language and can impart a message after a dog has left a particular area. Scent signals used in the marking of territory include the deposition of faeces, urine and glandular secretions, which also give an individual odour signature to each and every dog.

Leg cocking

This is one of the most obvious scent marking behaviours in male dogs. Small quantities of urine are left at numerous locations. This behaviour begins to occur as male dogs enter puberty but may also develop in similar form in bitches, particularly when coming on heat as part of a signalling system to show receptivity to mating. Dogs may spend a lot of their time on walks over-marking the marks of other dogs to denote their occupancy and usage of home ranges and to mask the odours of competitors. Many male dogs and, to a lesser extent, females may also

scratch the ground with their back feet after urinating or defecating, possibly to spread the scent or as a visual marker associated with the scent signal of the urine, and also possibly to deposit further scent secreted from glands on the sides of their footpads.

Vocal communication

Vocal signals enable dogs to communicate over long distances and in situations where visual signals may be inefficient, e.g. at night or in dense cover. Also, hearing a bark or a howl enables a dog to pin-point at distance roughly where the other dog is at the precise time of the signal, and so react immediately. Dogs have evolved from the wolf at the one time of its development when it is quite noisy and makes sounds similar to barks – the juvenile phase. Probably as a direct

GERMAN SHEPHERD DOG BODY LANGUAGE

German Shepherd Dogs are usually keen to interact with people and they are very enthusiastic communicators. Their body language and facial expressions usually make it easy for us to interpret their moods and intentions, and the position and movement of their tail and ears in particular enables your German Shepherd Dog to communicate a wide variety of emotions in a very obvious style. This alone is sufficient reason to condemn the practice of tail docking carried out in other breeds.

What greater signal of friendliness can there be than a German Shepherd Dog's wagging tail, or signal of disquiet than a dropped still tail, or of fear when the tail is held down between the legs? One of the joys of owning a German Shepherd is the ease of interpretation of his language through big eye, ear and facial movements and expressive movement and position of the tail, even if table-level house ornaments will need placing on shelves above dog level if they are to survive!

result of this, adult dogs bark far more than adult wolves and can develop a wide repertoire of vocal signals. Barks are used in defence of territory, in play and as an attention-seeking language in greeting, whereas low growls are used as warning and threat signals in social altercations, and a higher range of whimpers, whines and yips are used to deflect social challenges, and in excitable greetings.

Wolves howl to maintain contact with other members when physically isolated and unable to use direct language, and to rally the pack when out hunting, whereas dogs, with the exception of the chasing hounds, howl primarily as a signal of anxiety when left alone by their owners. Some breeds are noisier than others, and German Shepherds are certainly above average, with the ability and readiness to sound a very loud, deep guarding bark as required.

COMMUNICATING YOUR LEADERSHIP

Your dog views you perhaps somewhere between a parental figure and a packmate, from whom to expect signals of leadership and protection. Since you are also the packmate who provides food, initiates hunting excursions (walks!) and play, and defines sleeping areas, your role as director is reinforced regularly. A stable leader does not maintain his position by a regime of force, threat and punishment, but through communicating his strengths, will and moods effectively and safely to members of his group so that his right to lead is accorded to him by them. Understanding the social structure of a pack animal is simple – the higher up the ladder you are, the more privileges you are granted – but when dogs live in a mixed pack of humans and dogs, understanding the rules can be confusing.

The leader of the pack

Different breeds and types of dog organize their social structure in different ways, suggesting that there is a need for some to organize a social system between themselves and with their human pack mates. Some breeds seem rather unconcerned about having a leader of their pack, but most, including German Shepherd Dogs, seem to expect to live in a group with a leader. In any case, we normally expect to manage and dictate the dog's behaviour and lifestyle and so effectively appoint ourselves as leader and expect the dog to learn how to respond to our direction.

The simple procedures that are described below, once accepted by your dog, will help ensure that he responds more willingly to being trained, once he has learned the meaning of your signals, because he will respect your superior rank happily.

1 **Freedom of movement** It is the right of the high-ranking members of your pack, i.e. you and your family, to move about your shared den and rest and sleep where you wish, so try to deny your dog similar freedom of movement around the house and make upstairs, the centre of the den where you sleep, into a 'no go' area for him. This can be achieved by keeping some downstairs doors shut to keep him out of certain rooms for a few days until he accepts his new restricted access and by fitting a baby gate at the bottom of the stairs. By the same token, try not to allow the dog on your chairs and define his main sleeping area, at least, as one secure comfortable bed on the floor which you can remove or occupy if you wish.

2 **Social interaction** Make sure that all the benefits of social interaction for your dog, such as being stroked, fed, given treats, walked, played with etc., are usually initiated by you rather than your dog obtaining them from you on demand. How many times have you sat down, intent upon watching a television programme, when suddenly your hand is boldly pushed into the air by your dog wanting to be stroked? In most cases we respond immediately, partly because if we don't, we know that the dog will usually persevere until he gets stroked and interrupts our viewing, and partly because we want to be affectionate.

■ What may be happening in some cases is that the dog is dictating continually the order of our social relationship, deciding who is going to stroke him, when he will be stroked and for how long the interaction will continue. Calling him to you and making him sit and wait before stroking him puts you back in control without reducing the total time spent in contact, or the quality of your relationship.

■ In fact, this restructuring of the relationship and earning of desirable aspects of contact will communicate very quickly that you are the higher ranking animal and that it is worth your dog's while to wait for your signals. He should then learn consistently to approach you a little more cautiously and 'politely' when wanting affection or other rewarding contact, and then you will be able to respond to his modified approach without risk of elevating his status to the point where he wishes to dictate the order of life to you.

Don't feed your dog on demand – always initiate the feeding.

3 Feeding Top dogs usually eat first and subordinates must wait until the food source is vacated before gaining access, so sometimes it can help to prepare your dog's meals in his presence and then make him wait for them while you eat your meals. This may seem like teasing, especially to a ravenous puppy, but it instinctively tells him that at feeding times you get the best first – he gets the rest when you allow him access to his food bowl. This is especially important with puppies and young dogs as, weight for weight, they need to take in a lot more food relative to adult dogs in order to grow and so they can be taught new commands and come to accept their social position very well using manipulation of availability of food.

4 Strength games When young, most types of dog use possession of trophies to instigate ritualized forms of competition to help define their relative strength and handling skills and develop social relations with each other. Some dogs, such as retriever types, invariably continue to use possession of objects and toys as the main method of maintaining their social order as adults. 'Those who play together, stay together!'
■ It is important to play competitive strength games such as tug-o-war only if you are prepared to win them. This means that you must end up ultimately with the tug toy and keep possession by putting it somewhere out of the dog's reach. If you can't win when you wish, don't play this type of game with German Shepherds because they have a powerful jaw grip and are very strong in competition. All such games are best played outdoors where they seem to have less social significance.

5 Follow the leader Try to make sure that you usually go through narrow openings like doorways and passageways first and effectively lead your dog through. Encourage the dog to follow you, not lead or herd you through an open doorway. If he tries to push ahead, shut the door gently and block his path, repeating the procedure until he hesitates behind you and allows you to move unopposed.

6 Rights of passage Expect your dog to move out of your way when you move about the house – fitting a light trailing house line to the collar or Gentle Leader headcollar system (see page 45) for a few days allows you to do this easily. Call him to you when you need him and encourage him to move towards you for contact or attention rather than you going humbly to him.

CREATING EFFECTIVE COMMUNICATION

Of course, there are thousands of pet dogs who are being afforded some or all of these signals of authority on a daily basis, but they do not present a problem. They are perfectly biddable either because they are of a type that is not particularly status conscious, or all the hundreds of other signals that you give convey perfectly well to them that you are 'in charge', even if some of the behaviour can be contradictory in a canine sense. If your dog is not a problem in his control, training or behaviour and he comes to you for a cuddle, lies on your lap or sleeps in your bedroom, please do! But if you are having problems with your dog, these are the areas that you may have to change for these are some of the resources and signals that can affect a dog's perception of where he fits into your pack and what rights and responsibilities he may have in leading and directing you, rather than the other way round! For help with behaviour problems, contact a qualified pet behaviour counsellor (see page 144).

Training techniques

A well-trained dog is a pleasure to own but, to be effective, training should be enjoyable for both dog and owner. Dogs have suffered enormously, from the harsh training methods of old that far too

Training your dog to walk on the lead can be achieved with kindness and rewards.

38

A WORD OF CAUTION

■ It's very easy, given the right attitude and equipment, for you and your family to train your German Shepherd Dog to be a dog who responds happily to the usual everyday commands that most owners need for control. Training him to 'sit', 'stay', 'come', 'lie down', 'stay', 'come' and, most importantly, 'stop', is a simple question of associating each of the signals from you with the desired response and then reinforcing the conditioned response by rewarding the behaviour.

■ However, the traditional methods (shouting and punishing) of achieving these simple aims actually militate against the teaching process and cannot be justified now that we understand much more about how dogs learn. The use of loud voices, choke chains ('check chains') and physical punishment in dog training is increasingly a thing of the past, and modern educated trainers and behaviourists believe that using a choke chain is no longer an acceptable way to train a dog. They have found that threatening training techniques using such punishing methods can cause more physical and psychological harm than good; kinder methods based on motivational techniques are more effective.

many owners and unthinking dog trainers have regarded as normal and 'the way to do it' in local training classes for so many years.

■ **Choke chains** train dogs by teaching them avoidance behaviour through applying the punishment of pain or anticipated pain, so there can be no such thing as 'correct use' or justified use of a choke chain. Such methods can cause great physical damage and neck injuries are commonly seen by vets following the use of this equipment. But even if this is thankfully avoided, problems may develop in a dog's behaviour afterwards, including many forms of aggression brought about by fear and its associated high level of arousal. In any case, after being choked and checked and shouted at, the reactive, sensitive German Shepherd Dog's view of his owners, and perhaps mankind in general, may already have been damaged and their mutual relationship seriously undermined.

When to start training

For those seeking help with training their dog, it's essential to disregard another piece of traditional nonsense in the world of dogs: the debarring of dogs from some training classes until they are at least six months old. This is the very time when they are becoming more competitive and going through the difficult and distracting phase of adolescence! As with young children, the earlier that your German Shepherd Dog starts learning the better and, while the concentration span of a

six to eight-week-old puppy may be quite low, the sooner you start training him with the positive techniques and equipment outlined in this section, the better. Puppy classes, run by assessed and approved trainers, are designed specifically to help you with this and will take pups up to the age of about eighteen weeks, which is just before the onset of puberty when their behaviour also starts to be motivated by new hormonal influences.

Reward and non-reward

Our job in training dogs is to motivate them through the prospect of gaining rewards to behave as we wish them to by signalling our behaviour and intents effectively and clearly. Then a dog can not only interpret our requirements but also take comfort from a consistent, positive and happy relationship.

Signalling rewards in Pavlovian style is easy enough, and every dog learns very quickly that a smiling face, high voice and rattle of the biscuit tin is associated with a rewarding experience. However, a basic error that owners often make is to assume that 'punishment' is the opposite of 'reward' and that threatening or smacking a dog will decrease the frequency or expression of an unwanted behaviour. Not so. The opposite of reward is not punishment, but is 'non-reward', and letting your dog know this through a signal is just as easy as signalling rewards for behaviour that you do wish to encourage and teach your dog.

SIGNALLING REWARD AND NON-REWARD

Effective signalling of reward and non-reward is what will define your relationship together, establish you as the controlling influence, and encourage your dog to follow your lead happily. Before starting to train your German Shepherd Dog, it is important that you understand the difference between reinforcement and rewards.

REINFORCEMENT AND REWARD

A reinforcement, positive or negative, is something that happens when an act is occurring and is therefore seen to be received as a direct consequence for something that the dog is doing. Put simply, a positive reinforcement is anything that occurs during a particular act that the dog finds pleasant and so is likely to increase the possibility that the behaviour will be repeated. For example, a dog finds dropped scraps at the base of a child's high chair and quickly learns to take up a 'ready-to-forage' position as soon as the child is placed in it at mealtimes.

■ A reward is something that is positive and pleasurable to the dog and which usually happens after an act has occurred: a form of payment for a job well done. The only difference between a reward and a reinforcement is therefore in its timing.

■ However, a reward must be offered immediately after the behaviour that earned it in order for it to be clearly associated with the behaviour. Any delay in rewarding a specific action could result in subsequent unwanted behaviour being rewarded instead!

Intentional reward

Using intentional rewards in training does not require hours and hours of drill-type training, choke chains or harsh voices. It's simply a matter of letting your dog find out what he

Reward your dog's good behaviour immediately by praising him and offering a titbit.

needs to do in order to earn the reward.

■ For example, you can often teach your dog to sit on command by simply holding and showing him a titbit above his head, just out of reach, and then moving it slightly behind his head.

■ Ignore any efforts to snatch the titbit and close your hand if he makes a grab. Frustrated at not being able to obtain the titbit, he will usually try alternative behaviours but will soon sit down to get a better look at the food.

■ The instant his bottom hits the floor, say 'sit' to associate the word with the position and give him his reward. Next time he is presented with the titbit in similar circumstances, he will remember that he had to sit down in order to obtain it and after other similarly rewarding experiences will often sit without being asked when he sees the titbit.

■ He will have taught himself how to earn the reward; our job will have been simply to associate the word 'sit' with the behaviour so that we may use it more broadly and without always having to proffer a titbit.

Unintentional reward

We can sometimes encourage problems for ourselves by giving inadvertent or unintentional rewards to dogs. A good example of this can be seen in attention-demanding dogs. If a dog picks up one of his toys while we are on the phone, we ignore it. If he picks up one of our shoes, we interrupt the telephone conversation to tell him off and take the shoe away. As attention of any sort, be it scolding or praising, is seen as success, he repeats the behaviour next time the phone rings and one begins to wonder who is training whom? Such dogs are not intrinsically disobedient or problem dogs; in fact, they are usually very clever and certainly very good at training our behaviour.

SURVIVAL REWARD

The outcome of some behaviours reward a dog much more than anything we can offer. Dogs, as with all mammals, have one purpose in life and that is to remain fit and healthy in order to survive. To survive in challenges or conflicts they use one of the four 'F' strategies featured on page 30. For example, if a dog has not been socialized properly towards people when young, he may always be fearful of strangers as an adult and it may be his particular coping 'strategy' when confronted by a stranger is to threaten to 'fight' or actually to attack him. This policy usually results in the stranger backing off which, for the dog, functions as the reward! In effect, he thinks that he has 'saved his own life', an ultimate form of reward which quickly reinforces the use of aggression when confronted with similar circumstances in the future.

DOG TRAINING DISCS

The withdrawal or omission of an expected reward is known as 'non-reward'. This causes frustration in dogs and other animals and, as one would expect, the greater the expected reward, the greater the frustration. But when a sound or other signal is introduced as a signal of non-reward, this in itself does not induce frustration. The animal

A German Shepherd Dog and Training Discs.

withdraws from the warning signal and this action actually becomes a reward because it reduces his frustration. This is known as 'passive avoidance' and, through it, dogs learn to refrain from behaviours which lead to unrewarding or unpleasant prospects. Dog Training Discs were developed by the canine behaviourist John Fisher to enable owners to signal 'non-reward' and thus encourage calm resignation in a dog when confronted with something that previously made him over-excited or made him behave 'badly' from his owner's point of view.

■ **Dog Training Discs** are five brass discs on a fob which, when shaken, make a rather unique sound. However, it is not the sound itself but the introductory process of the discs which makes them so effective in training dogs and treating problem behaviour.

■ The introduction involves presenting the dog with an expected reward and then calmly removing it as he approaches it. This is usually performed by dropping a few favoured titbits on the floor. The dog will move to take the titbits, intentions and behaviours which he sees as potentially rewarding.

■ The owner or trainer then drops the discs near the dog fractionally before

USING THE DISCS SUCCESSFULLY

Dogs do not get used to the sound or learn to ignore the discs provided they are introduced properly and away from any particular problem behaviour to establish them as a clear signal of non-reward. Because the sound is consistent in tone, it can be used effectively by any member of the family. Once the dog is conditioned to respond to the discs, he will react promptly in a similar way to any signal of reward. Because the success of the response depends on individual conditioning, the discs are not recommended for use within a dog training club environment and, ideally, owners of more than one dog should use the discs as the conditioning signal only for one of their dogs and employ other similarly introduced sounds for the others. For deaf dogs, a camera flashlight, introduced in the same way as the discs, yields just as effective results although its scope outdoors during daylight is obviously limited.

lifting the titbits away as the dog stoops down to eat them.

■ After four or five repetitions, the dog learns that the sound of the discs is a signal of 'frustrative non-reward' or failure of his intents to take and eat the titbits.

■ The dog may look a little confused and frustrated at his failure to gain the titbits and usually turns to his owners for some reassurance. This should be offered immediately, as comfort from the owner is a safety signal that helps relieve the dog's frustration at having failed in his previous intentions.

■ This introduction procedure teaches the dog a passive avoidance response – in future, he will not even attempt to move towards the titbits whenever he hears the sound. But this is only the introduction procedure. The sound of the discs can now be used to help to interrupt any unwanted actions on the part of the dog, e.g. barking excitedly at people in enthusiastic greetings (a notable German Shepherd trait!) and to overcome a variety of previously learned unwanted behaviours, such as chasing bicycles and joggers. When the dog hears the sound, he avoids completing the behaviour he was intent on and returns quietly to his owner.

■ Because he is automatically in a relaxed state, he can be encouraged to perform a different behaviour, such as coming to them walking by their side when bicycles or joggers pass: a calm interactive behaviour which can then be rewarded. After a couple of interruptions with the discs, as they leap up or bark at visitors, even the noisiest and most excitable of German Shepherd Dogs soon learn to approach people more calmly and are easily persuaded to sit and wait to be patted instead.

THE GENTLE LEADER SYSTEM

This was first developed in the United States in the early 1980s by top veterinarian Professor Bob Anderson and Ruth Foster, a former President of the National Association of Obedience Instructors. The Gentle Leader is a comfortable nylon headcollar which is designed specifically for dogs, and which adapts to fit the contours of each individual dog's face. This scientific concept in the control, training and management of dogs has been designed specially to help the owners mimic the way that dogs naturally communicate and has a unique mode of action that takes account of canine behaviour.

How the Gentle Leader works

Dogs have a natural instinct to pull against pressure and dogs walked on choke or regular collars still pull, even though pressure on the throat causes pain and choking and even though their owners may yank, tug and shout to try and stop them. The Gentle Leader does not choke a dog. It is designed scientifically to direct the dog's entire body by controlling his head and nose, in the same way that man has controlled horses and other livestock for centuries, but it also helps dissuades him from pulling on the lead by transferring

The Gentle Leader headcollar is comfortable to wear and a valuable training aid.

45

some of his forward energy to the back of his neck via the neckstrap when he tries to pull forwards. Puppies instinctively relax when their mother picks them up and pressure is applied to the scruff of their necks. This is a natural adaptation for survival as it enables her to transport them with minimal fuss to escape from threats.

The Gentle Leader therefore gives owners natural effective leadership, kind control and 'power steering'. It is recommended especially for controlling boisterous dogs and puppies, and for all dogs that pull on the lead, and enables owners to train their dogs at home and outdoors to be sociable and obedient, calmly, quickly and effectively. At home or in training classes, all you will need aside from the Gentle Leader is your dog's usual lead, a supply of his favourite small titbits or a favourite toy to use as rewards, along with a positive, happy and rewarding attitude and a little patience, especially with young dogs. Its success in producing over one million happy well-trained dogs in the States and rapidly increasing numbers in the UK and Europe since its full launch in 1994 is a testament to its excellent patented design and application for dogs and their owners.

BASIC TRAINING

The ideal place to begin to train your puppy or older dog is where he is most relaxed: at home and in the garden. Once he has learned the signals of reward and non-reward and grown accustomed to wearing his lead, collar and Gentle Leader, follow the simple procedures below. Once he has grasped the basics, take him to a wide range of new places and repeat the plan so that your puppy or dog comes to behave calmly and accept your instructions everywhere you are together.

1 Stopping pulling on the lead

■ If your dog walks or pulls ahead of you, use the lead to turn the dog's nose (not his body) around and up so it points directly towards your eyes.

■ Keep walking forwards, taking up slack on the lead to maintain tension, even if your dog pulls backwards or sits.

■ When you reach your dog's side, praise him and encourage him to walk next to you. To keep him at your side and to prevent him pulling ahead, anticipate his action and gently raise his nose as soon as his shoulder passes your leg. Your dog's instinctive response will make him halt momentarily to relieve the pressure on the back of his neck, and this will cause him to slow down and stop pulling.

■ Walk on immediately with more words of encouragement. Never jerk the lead or tell your dog off if he is a little slow to learn what you want of him – this will frighten him and make him even slower. Instead, simply repeat the above in gentle fashion until he understands how to walk calmly beside you without pulling ahead.

2 Walking/jogging to heel

■ Stand to one side of your dog and hold the lead in your hand, leaving a maximum of 5 cm/2 in of slack where it joins the lead attachment ring under his chin. Fold any excess lead into your other hand.

■ Talk to your dog with a friendly, encouraging voice and start walking forwards. If your dog holds back, keep walking forwards, coaxing him with kind words and perhaps the motivating offer of sight of a favourite toy or titbit.

■ At the same time, pull gently forwards on the lead and release the tension as soon as he sets off. Your dog will soon learn that good things happen when he comes to your side.

■ Begin by asking him to 'walk' and set off walking at your normal pace, keeping him at your side. Then ask him to 'run' while steadily increasing your pace to a gentle trot, keeping him by your side and always speaking to him encouragingly. Increase slowly to your normal jogging pace, encouraging him to 'jog' as you go. He'll soon associate the three words with your three different paces. You might also like to teach him to 'slow' as you want to slow down so that he doesn't run on uncomfortably and pull on ahead after you've decided to stop!

BASIC TRAINING

3 'Sit'

■ Hold the lead in your right hand. Pull it forwards and upwards to point your dog's nose gently skywards. As you tip his nose up, his head should go gently back and his hindquarters will lower to the ground.

■ As soon as his hindquarters touch the ground, say 'sit' in an encouraging voice and immediately release the tension on the lead and allow his head to move freely, and offer him a titbit. He may stand up again immediately especially if he is young, but repeat several times and he will soon associate the sitting

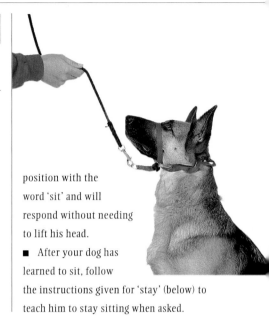

position with the word 'sit' and will respond without needing to lift his head.

■ After your dog has learned to sit, follow the instructions given for 'stay' (below) to teach him to stay sitting when asked.

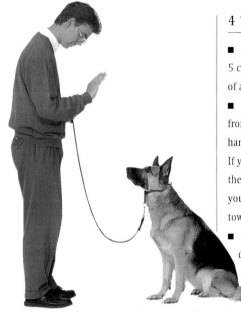

4 'Stay'

■ Holding the lead in your left hand with 5 cm (2 in) of slack, you should hold a reward of a titbit or toy in your right hand.

■ Give the command 'stay' from directly in front of the dog, raising the palm of your right hand to face him, while still holding the titbit. If your dog tries to move forwards or to take the reward, pull up gently on the lead with your left hand, at the same time moving towards the dog repeating the command 'stay'.

■ After a few seconds, move towards your dog and reward his patience by lowering your right hand to give him the titbit or toy and praise him.

- Gradually increase the 'stay' time until your dog has learned to 'stay' for a minute or so. You may then wish to extend the distance between you, so walk slowly backwards with the palm of your right hand raised to face him while repeating the 'stay' command until you have reached the length of the lead. If your dog moves towards you, remind him to 'stay' by pulling gently up on the lead with your left hand and then quickly releasing it. Begin again from close by, repeating the command 'stay'.
- To extend the distance beyond the length of the lead, retreat to its full extent, lay it on the ground and continue to retreat slowly with your palm raised and facing your dog as before while you repeat the 'stay' command.
- When you decide he has remained in the 'stay' long enough, return to him calmly and reward and praise him – do not call him to you to be rewarded for the stay, or you will be rewarding the 'come'. Gradually increase the time you expect him to remain in the 'stay' and steadily lengthen the distance away from you in small stages.

5 'Down'

- Teach 'down' while your dog is in the 'sit' position at your left side. Hold a toy or food reward in your hand about 2.5 cm (1 in) in front of his nose.
- With his nose following the reward, bring your hand slowly down to the floor and, while saying 'down', move the object slowly away from the dog at floor level to induce him to lie down. Do not push down on your dog's back as he will push back up and resist going 'down'.
- Sometimes you can encourage him to obey the 'down' command by drawing the reward under a low table so that he must go down underneath it in order to get to the reward.

BASIC TRAINING

- Repeat the command 'down' as soon as he adopts the correct position. After your dog has learned 'down', follow the instructions for 'stay' to teach him to stay down.

- When your dog is lying down, reward him with a toy or a food titbit.

6 'Come'

- To maintain your leadership/control during training, attach your dog's lead to the Gentle Leader so that you can control the distance between you and your dog as you teach, so that your dog can never run away from you when you give the command 'come'.

An extending lead is useful to extend the range of training this response.

- Begin with your dog sitting in front of you. Place a favourite toy or titbit on the palm of your hand. Kneel on one knee to lower your profile and offer less potential threat.

- Extend your forearm and your hand showing the reward, giving the command 'come' with an enthusiastic gentle voice. Your dog should be eager to respond to your request. As he steps towards you, say 'good dog' as praise and show your hand, palm up, for the dog to take the reward.

■ Your dog will only have to take a step forwards to gain his reward initially, but as soon as he learns to come when called, extend the distance between you to a pace or two and then steadily further away, repeating the whole process at each increase. Do not proceed too fast too far, or the dog may fail to obey and get distracted.

■ If that happens, gently pull on the lead to turn his head towards you, but quickly release the tension as soon as you have his attention. Then get your dog's attention again, offer the reward and repeat the command 'come'. If the dog still doesn't want to come, reduce the distance between you and start again. After your dog is responding again at a short distance, gradually increase the distance again.

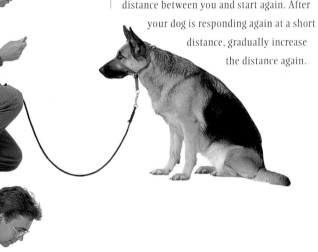

PART TWO

CARING FOR YOUR DOG

Buying a dog is one of the most important decisions you will make, and it is important that you do so only after careful thought and consideration. The dog will become your constant companion for the next ten to fifteen years so not only must you choose the right puppy but also you must learn how to care for your dog on a daily basis and make time to exercise, feed and play with him.

Owning a dog is pleasurable and rewarding and can add a new dimension to your life as long as you are prepared to make the commitment to training, socialization and all the other aspects of everyday care.

In the following pages, you will find practical advice on finding a puppy and looking after him as well as care of the adult dog. Never be tempted to buy on impulse – remember that a dog is for life.

CHAPTER THREE

THE GERMAN SHEPHERD PUPPY

CHOOSING A PUPPY

Buying any puppy is a huge responsibility. Caring for any breed of dog takes time, energy and money – all precious resources that very few of us have in abundance. German Shepherds are traditionally one of our favourite pets. Renowned for their devotion and loyalty, they are also famous for their intelligence and working abilities as police dogs, service dogs, sniffer dogs, rescue dogs and guide dogs. However, the image of the German Shepherd Dog as a

YOUR LIFESTYLE

Take some time to think about your lifestyle. All puppies and dogs need company. They are social animals and their ancestral heritage means most of them find it difficult to be isolated from the rest of their pack. Wolves are rarely alone from the moment of birth to the moment of death, and so leaving any dog at home alone requires training and understanding to enable him to learn to cope. If your family is out all day, think again about getting any kind of dog.

highly-trained working animal may not give us the whole story as far as pet ownership is concerned. Like many other large breeds of dog, they consume vast amounts of food, need a great deal of exercise once adult and require a well above average commitment to socialization and training.

They are adaptable dogs and, in the right environment, blossom into good companions, but do you really have the space, financial commitment and time for this kind of dog? Shepherds look lithe and graceful giving demonstrations of agility and their working skills. However, they are just as likely to want to expend this energy if cooped up in a small environment – and this means they are not ideally suited to life in a flat or in a small house with no garden, unless you can offer them sufficient stimulation and exercise outside these confines.

Over-attachment

German Shepherds are also particularly prone to becoming over-attached to one

person or one member of the family. While this may be fine if you live alone and have few friends, for most of us that means recognising a huge commitment to socializing the puppy with large numbers of people both inside and outside the home, and for needing the co-operation of all the family to share the dog's daily responsibilities.

German Shepherds are known for their undying affection and loyalty to

German Shepherds make good pets although there is a danger of them becoming over-attached to one person.

their nearest and dearest. However, it should not be underestimated that the breed is large and powerful, and that many people are now cautious of dogs they meet in the park or on the street. All large, so-called 'guarding' breeds have come under a lot of pressure from the general media. Although much of this bad press is exaggerated and unrealistic, we must accept that not everyone is a dog lover. The only way to stem the growing tide of fearful or antagonistic reactions to dogs in our society is to prove by example that large dogs such as German Shepherds can be gentle, loving and kindly when they are well-socialized and well-trained.

Working or pet?

German Shepherds do not only come in two different coat lengths, but they also vary in colour. Although the long-coats are regarded by serious competitors and breeders as 'undesirable' and are unlikely to win prizes in any beauty contests, their appeal is undeniable. However, far more important than external appearance is the dog's character and temperament. If you are looking for a family pet that will be happy to fit in with an average exercise routine and lots of contact with visitors, children and other dogs while out on walks, do not buy from a line of security dogs or guarding types! All dogs will do a good job of barking at the door when a stranger arrives – there is absolutely no need to buy what is essentially a pet dog from a breeder who specializes in guard dogs.

When buying a puppy, insist on seeing the mother in order to observe her behaviour and temperament.

FINDING THE RIGHT DOG

If you have decided that a German Shepherd is the pet for you – you have the time, energy, money and the commitment – you need to go about finding one that will suit your needs.

Finding a breeder

Finding a breeder who has puppies for sale is always best done through a responsible outlet. Some organisations now have lists of breeders who agree to abide by an ethical code of practice – that they have tested their stock for any hereditary diseases and have raised their puppies in ideal conditions.

■ Don't be tempted to buy a puppy from an advert in a newspaper, particularly where more than one breed is included for sale, or from a local pet shop. Many are outlets for puppy farms where unscrupulous people breed puppies en masse in appalling conditions and without the necessary care over the health or temperament of their breeding stock or with any thought to socialization.

■ Always insist on seeing the mother and, even better, the father too when choosing a puppy. The mother's temperament and behaviour have an enormous influence on the puppies. Of course, the father gives fifty per cent of his genes and characteristics too, but very often a breeder may take a bitch to be mated to a stud dog that lives some distance away and is therefore not around to be seen.

■ Never buy a puppy spontaneously, and never be tempted to buy from anyone who offers to deliver the puppy to you, or to meet you half-way to exchange the puppy at a service station.

HEREDITARY DISEASES

Always insist on seeing the scores for hereditary diseases of both parents when buying a German Shepherd. Sadly, they suffer from hip dysplasia, (which can lead to lameness, loss of use of the back legs, or chronic arthritis), PRA (progressive retinal atrophy – progressive and incurable blindness), OCD (malformation of the cartilage that makes movement and exercise painful) and pancreas problems. There is also a history of epilepsy in the breed. See the Healthcare section (page 94).

Home comforts

■ Although it may be heart-breaking, never, ever, be tempted to buy a puppy which has not been born in the home of the person selling it. German Shepherds need constant socializing. Puppies that have been born outside the home environment, in a barn or shed, or even some of those born in immaculate kennels at the bottom of the breeder's garden, cannot have experienced enough of everyday life and contact with people, children and domestic environmental stimuli, such as the vacuum cleaner or the TV, and are unlikely to cope with them in later life. Steel yourself, and walk away from any puppies that have not been born and raised in the home, especially if the mother is not available to see, or if her temperament is unsound.

■ A mother of good temperament will be happy to see visitors and children, and will be confident enough in her environment and owners to allow you to play with and pick up her puppies. Any mother that backs away, growls, snarls or appears in any way nervous, aggressive

SOCIALIZATION

Puppies go through various stages of development, the most crucial being the socialization period, from three to twelve weeks, when much of your puppy's adult behaviour and character will be determined. As more than half of this time is likely to be spent with the breeder, it is critical that this is not wasted, or ruined by bad experiences.

Of course, you need to continue with your puppy's socialization once you have brought him home, but it is difficult to make up for what happens to the puppy prior to the eight-week stage.

or subdued may have passed these traits to her puppies. Do not take the risk – you will be the one to pay for it later.

■ Be prepared for the breeder to ask you lots of questions about your lifestyle and the commitment you can give to your puppy. Some may even want to see photographs of your garden! This is not an attempt to check out your gardening abilities or be nosy about your personal life; it shows a caring and responsible attitude towards the future of the puppy. Be suspicious if the only question asked is how you would like to pay.

■ With this in mind, it may be that you have to wait for the right puppy from the right breeder to be born. However, joy from your dog for the next fifteen or so years is worth waiting for now.

■ The more a puppy experiences before you even bring him home, the more confident, outgoing and steady he is likely to be as a juvenile and an adult. Thus the one-off pet dog breeders can sometimes be your best bet. As long as they are not attempting to breed for profit and the bitch is a confident, friendly much-loved family pet, there is much to be said for a litter of puppies that have been played with by the children, handled by visitors, played in the garden and taken on car rides.

WHICH ONE FOR YOU?

Choosing a puppy to be an ideal pet from a litter is not an easy task. Obviously, if you have a preference for choosing a dog or a bitch this will narrow your choice. Usually, females are easier to train and are less competitive in a family environment than males. However, both will require the same amount of veterinary treatment, socialization, exercise, training and general care. Colour or coat preferences may also restrict your choice. It is possible that long-coats are easier to socialize with other people while a smooth-coated puppy may already look 'adult' to those who are anxious about approaching dogs.

Pick an average pup

Probably the most important factor to look for when choosing a puppy as a pet is to pick the most average! Many people report that their puppy chose them, by running up, pushing all the other puppies out of the way, and demanding their attention. This may well be the puppy to choose if you want to enter working trials, obedience or agility competitions with your dog, but as the family pet this same dog may be ruling the roost within two months of settling in at home!

Equally unsuitable is the puppy that does not want to approach you, and sits at the back of the litter, or hides behind its mother or litter-mates. Some dogs like this may turn out to be highly intelligent and quick to learn – they usually have to use brain rather than brawn. However, the risks of problems of nervousness or anxiety are increased.

One or two puppies?

At this stage, be sensible and try not to be overcome by the cuteness of the puppies in front of you. If you are in any doubt, leave them there! A good breeder should be happy for you to think about your decision, and then come back to see the puppies again if necessary, rather than rushing you to make a decision.

■ Do not be tempted to take two pups at the same time, even if your heart is breaking at the thought of leaving one puppy behind on his own. Two puppies of the same age, particularly litter-mates, are a recipe for disaster! It is vital that

THE IDEAL PET

The puppy that is happy to see you, to be picked up, handled and played with, is not overly daunted by a sudden sound, such as a hand-clap, and plays well with its litter-mates, is likely to be the most well-balanced ideal pet dog.

we understand that although dogs settle well and live in harmony with a human social group, we are a different species. One dog in a human social group learns to interact and communicate with us to be able to survive, and this is where the man/dog bond is formed. Put two dogs together into such an environment from day one and they will interact more with each other, often to the exclusion of humans, and sometimes to the exclusion even of other types of dog.

■ If you have already decided that you would like two dogs, be patient and wait until you have formed a relationship, socialized and trained one dog through to adolescence, all of which takes a surprising length of time, and then think about getting another. Two puppies together are rarely double the joy – only double the trouble!

Choose an average puppy which is neither over-confident nor nervous.

WHAT AGE?

The time at which most breeders allow puppies to leave their mother and go to a new home varies enormously. Puppies need to stay in their own litter and with their mother to learn about dog language – how dogs interact with each other socially – and to be taught vital information by their mother. During the first few weeks of life, puppies play a great deal with each other in the litter, practising how it feels to win contests for food, toys or attention and experimenting with body language which they will later recognise as signals of intent connected with dominance, submission, appeasement, pacification, possession and rejection.

■ **Weaning** is the time when puppies learn to cope with frustration by experiencing rejection by the mother. However, during this time, it is vital that puppies learn about people – that some of our body language is different to theirs, and that we are friendly and non-threatening. Socialization with people must start early in the breeder's home. No puppy should be removed from the litter before it is six weeks old, and no later than eight weeks.

Puppies love to play and to win contests with their litter-mates or owners.

■ There is some controversy about what should happen during this two-week gap. Some behaviourists think that puppies are best brought into a human family environment as soon as possible, at six weeks of age, and certainly many guide dog organizations have been following this routine with success for many years. However, the fact that most puppies will not be able to have contact with other puppies of the same age for at least the next four weeks, because their vaccination programmes may not be complete, may mean that it is better for them to be left in the canine educational sector – the litter – until eight weeks, so that they can learn the rules and signals of canine communication. Certainly, a compromise needs to be reached. Dogs that have not had sufficient contact with humans prior to eight weeks are likely to be prone to behavioural problems connected with people, whereas those

THE IDEAL AGE

Of course, the absolute ideal – and one that should be available to everyone who is buying a puppy – should be that breeders provide enough human contact and environmental stimuli to allow the puppies to remain with their mother and litter-mates until they are eight weeks old.

In an ideal world, puppies would be exposed to the educational effects of their mother, and father, other well-balanced dogs, which are tolerant of puppies but do not allow them to take liberties, and hoards of people – all with friendly intentions! If only we lived in such a world.

given lots of human contact but taken too early from the litter are likely to have missed out on canine company and may display aggression to other dogs later on in life.

PLANNING FOR THE PUPPY'S ARRIVAL

Bringing your puppy home is exciting, particularly if you have had to wait for some time for the right puppy. A little planning before the excitement sets in is a good idea, particularly if you have a long journey ahead of you, another dog at home to whom you are going to introduce your new puppy, a cat, or another pet. First impressions count for a great deal, and the last thing you want is for the puppy to be worried or upset.

1 Ideally, take a piece of cloth or an old towel with you to the breeder's home when you visit your puppy or make final arrangements. Ask the breeder to put this under the mother's blankets, or in her bed, so that it will be covered with her scent when you bring it home with the pup. You can also do a 'scent exchange', by making sure the cloth or towel already has some of your scent on it (putting it in the laundry bin or under your bed sheet usually has this effect) so that your puppy will already be familiar with your scent before he comes home.

2 Prepare your car for the journey home, particularly if it is going to be a long drive. A large cardboard box or a bundle of towels are good ideas. You will need someone to help out by looking after the puppy in the back of the car for you if you are driving and, as puppies

THE PUPPY'S BED

Puppies chew absolutely everything at
this stage, so it is probably not worth
investing huge amounts on an expensive
bed. Puppies prefer the security of a
small cosy nest rather than a vast
expanse of bed to begin with, so a large
cardboard box, lined with a cosy blanket
is ideal. Wrapping the towel which has
been impregnated with the mother's and
litter-mates' familiar smells around a
warm hot water bottle, provides snug
security for your puppy.

usually have the habit of being sick on
long car journeys, towels and clean-up
tissues are a useful measure!

3 Make sure you have as much
information as possible from the
breeder before you pick up your puppy.
You will need to have bought the puppy
some of the food he is already used to eating, booked the puppy for his vaccination
jabs, found a local puppy socialization
class, checked out when you next need to
give worming tablets, planned where he
is going to sleep, and have a lightweight
collar and lead ready and waiting.

4 Puppies vary greatly in their
response to being taken away from
their mother and litter-mates and
brought into a new environment. Some
pups are bold and confident and walk

in as if they are already at home. Others
are more shy and require some quiet
time with the opportunity to explore at
their own pace. Try to discourage
children from overwhelming the puppy
at this stage. Even a confident puppy
may be a little daunted if he is
constantly being fussed, picked up
or touched.

Meeting other dogs

Most young puppies are cautious about
meeting new creatures, such as an older
dog or a cat, but some forethought will
help this to go as smoothly as possible.
First, it is up to the humans in the family
constantly to remind an established older
dog that he still has pride of place and is
boss of all he surveys. Making the
mistake of telling the older dog off for
trying to sniff the puppy or, later, for
reprimanding it, can seriously damage
the two dogs' future relationship.

If your established dog is generally
good with other dogs and puppies, it is
ideal to allow him to meet the puppy off
home territory; this is safest in the
garden, not in the street or park. Allow
your established dog as much free rein as
possible to investigate the newcomer. Try
to ignore the puppy, but praise and talk to
your older dog all the time he is showing
gentle interest. Allow your older dog to
walk into the house first, and follow
with the puppy. It is essential that you

establish recognition of the puppy as a subordinate to your older dog straight away. Roles may be reversed later on, but initially the puppy must not be put in a position where he appears to be competing for your attention.

■ Food is a valuable resource to a dog and an older dog may defend it if the puppy comes too close – so exercise some caution at meal times.

■ At other times, it is always best not to interfere if your older dog disciplines the puppy, as long as he is not actually damaging him.

■ If you are worried about your older dog's reaction to a newcomer in his house, use the protection of the puppy's play pen or crate to introduce the dogs – a safety cage is essential where the response of the older established dog is an unknown quantity.

■ If you know that your older dog is not friendly with other dogs, seek advice from a behaviour counsellor regarding your older dog's behaviour before making the decision to get another dog. All relationships in the household suffer when dogs refuse to get on together.

Cats and other pets

Introducing a puppy to a cat in the household is also an important part of making sure harmony reigns. The vital elements are to allow your cat a clear escape route or vantage point to jump up on, without allowing your puppy to experience the thrill of the chase. Generally, a cat that is confident around dogs will quickly establish itself as boss.

■ Introductions should be made with the puppy restrained, by being held on the floor, with the cat free to escape if necessary. The cat's food and water should be put out of the puppy's reach, and the puppy should be prevented from ambushing the cat while compromised

---

MAKE TIME FOR YOUR PUPPY

As the owner of two dogs, it is now vitally important that you set aside sufficient time to give individually to your new puppy. Most puppies bond extremely quickly to a tolerant older dog, and while it is rewarding to watch them play together and their relationship develop, it should not be to the exclusion of your own relationship with your dog. Most owners of two dogs report that their first dog has managed to communicate all the habits they wish he didn't have to the second one – and none of the good!

Unfortunately for us, dogs do not train themselves, or each other, and it is vital that you build an equally individual relationship with the second dog as the first. This means devoting a huge amount of time and energy to your puppy, away from his new canine friend, alone with you, and in the company of other dogs.

THE GERMAN SHEPHERD PUPPY

on the litter tray.

■ If introduced young enough, puppies can be taught to regard many other kinds of pets as being part of the family. However, caution and careful introductions are needed initially, and the puppy should be as young as possible to accept that other creatures such as guinea pigs, hamsters and rabbits are not prey animals, but are part of his 'pack'.

Your puppy can be left safely for short periods in a play pen with his bed and some chews and toys.

Play pens and crates

If there is one piece of equipment that is likely to save your sanity over the first few weeks of puppy ownership, it is an indoor kennel, which is sometimes called a crate, or, even better, a mesh play pen. Puppies need huge amounts of sleep to begin with, and although they may appear to be constantly energetic, they suddenly flop down and take a nap. This, and the fact that we cannot supervise them all the time, makes a play pen an absolute essential in terms of allowing us to relax, without worrying that if the puppy is quiet it must be up to something! Most puppies will happily chew through television cables and telephone wires if unsupervised and this can lead to stress all round. Far from being a cage to incarcerate your puppy when he has done wrong, a play pen or crate, if introduced

gradually and associated with pleasant things such as food or toys, is regarded by the dog as a cosy den – a secure area where he knows he won't be disturbed.

House-training

Using a crate also facilitates speedy house-training. This can be quick and painless for all concerned, and need never involve any form of punishment. Young puppies cannot be expected to have total control over their bodily functions, and the occasional accident is to be expected. By using an approach called 'errorless learning', puppies quickly learn what is expected of them.

■ **Errorless learning** means never allowing your puppy to make a mistake by going to the toilet in the wrong place. You can learn to predict when your puppy will need to go – usually this is after playing, after waking up, after any kind of excitement and immediately after meals. At these times, take your puppy to the same place outside and wait with him.

■ Gently repeating a phrase, e.g. 'Be quick', helps your puppy to remember why he's there. As soon as he starts to sniff around, or circle, praise him gently, but genuinely. When he has finished, praise him lavishly and give him a titbit to reward him. Don't rush him indoors immediately. Play for a while first, so that he doesn't delay in future in order to stay outdoors. In between these events, it is wise to take your puppy outside about once an hour, just in case he should need to go, and to watch him closely for signs such as sniffing or circling.

■ If you wait outside with your puppy and he does nothing, bring him back inside. At this point you know that he has not relieved himself and is likely to do so in the near future. It is then up to you to supervise him constantly. If you cannot watch him during that time, you either need to put him in the crate or play pen, or in an enclosed area where you do not mind if he has an accident.

DON'T GET ANGRY

Being cross with your puppy for making a mistake in the house is pointless. Dogs soon learn to associate any mess with your anger – not with the act of going – and simply show fear when you find it. The expression 'he knows what he has done – he even looks guilty' really means that the dog is showing fear when you are around. Dogs do not feel guilty for what they have done – they just learn to be scared of the consequences of your presence.

The advantage of confining your puppy for short periods when you cannot supervise him is that most dogs do not want to soil their sleeping area, and will try to wait until you take them out again.

■ If you catch your puppy in the act of going, or about to go, at any other time, say 'Outside' in an urgent voice, then take him quickly outside to show him where you do want him to go. If you get even one drop in the right place you can then praise your puppy.

■ It takes years for a child to be fully toilet trained, but no one would consider punishing a baby for having an accident in an inappropriate place. Old-fashioned punishments, such as rubbing the dog's nose in his own mess, are not only abhorrent but also counter-productive and should never be used.

■ Many people use sheets of newspaper to teach their puppy to go to the toilet where they want them to, but compared with the 'errorless' approach this is harder work in the long term, as you need to house-train your puppy twice – once to paper, and then again, outdoors.

■ Puppies that leak urine when meeting new people or dogs, or when greeting the family, are not showing a lack of house-training, but are communicating their deference in a submissive way. Puppies may roll over, sit with one hind leg held out to the side, or squirm along the floor when meeting someone or something they regard as being a little over-dominating, and they may accompany this with urinating, too. Ignoring the

puppy until you get outside, or crouching down and greeting the puppy side-on, without looking at him directly, often helps as it reassures the puppy that you are calm, gentle and friendly.

Lonely nights

During the first few nights that the puppy is away from his mother and litter-mates, it is likely that he will cry out if he feels lonely and isolated in the dark.

■ Traditionally, pet owners were told to ignore this crying and not to return to the dog to prevent establishing bad habits from day one. However, modern thought relies more on understanding the dog's behaviour as a social animal and the fact that he is crying through distress and anxiety, and not being 'naughty'.

■ Most puppies settle happily into their new home if they are not totally isolated from the family, and this is where compromise is required. If you have a pen or crate for your puppy, allowing him to be in the bedroom with you for a few nights is not a problem, as you can avoid any mess, give your puppy some reassurance by your physical proximity and

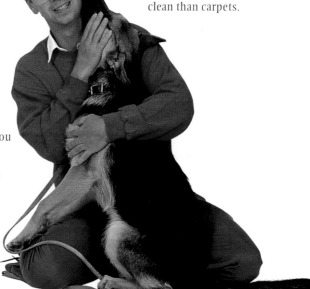

know when he needs to be taken outside.

■ Try not to respond to your puppy's every whimper – you do not want to teach him to cry for attention. At this stage it might be also be tempting to give in and allow your cuddly pup to snuggle under the duvet with you, but this is not advisable – unless you will be happy to continue doing this once your puppy has grown into an adult dog!

■ When your puppy has overcome the novelty of his new surroundings, and is beginning to form a bond with the family, he should be confident enough to be moved downstairs to sleep. This is more practical as being able to control the bladder and bowels for the whole night is something that comes gradually, and most kitchen floors are easier to clean than carpets.

CARING FOR YOUR PUPPY

Food and diet

Most German Shepherds have good appetites, and although some are finicky eaters, this is often a ploy to see whether they can train their owner to go back to the supermarket to buy something else! Of course, all puppies like food, and this not only makes them easy to feed, but also easy to train using reward-based, motivational methods.

Most reputable breeders provide new pet owners with a diet sheet as a guide to the pup's requirements over the following weeks. However, much confusion arises over these sheets, with owners not realising that more, less, or different food should be given as the dog grows, and that the sheet should be adapted to the individual dog's requirements.

There are many different types of leads, including heavy chains and ropes. A lightweight lead (centre) is most suitable for a puppy.

COLLARS AND LEADS

All dogs are required to wear both a collar and identification disc when out and about. It is a good idea to get your puppy used to wearing a very soft, lightweight collar as soon as possible, and then to sometimes attach a very light lead to it as well, in order that the strange feeling of something around the neck is introduced gradually. Some excellent nylon collars are now available, which allow you to expand the collar as the puppy grows, meaning that you don't have to keep buying additional collars in the next size up.

An extending lead is useful in training.

EARLY LEARNING

Puppies love to learn. They are just like little sponges absorbing information about their environment, the people around them, what feels good, and what does not. Traditionally, dogs had to wait until they were six months old before starting any kind of training. This was largely because old-fashioned training methods were too harsh for younger puppies. However, the advent of modern 'hands-off' methods of training, where the dog is motivated by food treats or toys and is not forced physically to comply, means that by waiting until your puppy is six months old you have missed the easiest time to train and socialize him.

Socialization classes

Puppy socialization classes are essential for your puppy. German Shepherds need significant amounts of contact with other puppies of a similar age, mainly because they have a very specific way of attempting to engage other dogs in play. They need lots of opportunities to learn about other dogs' body language and social graces – as early as possible!

■ Even at only twelve to fourteen weeks old, they can be very vocal, barking or growling to get other dogs' attention, and sometimes lunging out at dogs, or even people, in an attempt to catch them in an open-mouthed gape. This is not aggressive behaviour; it is an attempt to start a play session, or get the other dog moving. Most German Shepherds are hesitant when meeting other breeds. Initially, they tend to react as if they must try to dominate other dogs by shoulder-barging them, putting their heads over other dogs' necks, or barking, all of which can deter other dogs from wanting to play.

INOCULATION

Because of the risks of the various diseases that affect dogs, it is important that your puppy is inoculated against them. However, this inevitably means a delay in being able to take your puppy out to mix freely with other dogs, as he will need to have completed his vaccination programme before you can do so.

■ Try to find a vet who will provide the earliest possible vaccination programme for your puppy – the timing of the final injection still varies enormously, but your puppy should not be more than twelve weeks old at the stage where he can be safely taken out.

■ Prior to this time, if you can't take the puppy to the outside world, invite the outside world in to meet your puppy! Expose him early on to as many different people and experiences as possible.

A puppy class with some controlled off-lead play is therefore an absolute essential, as German Shepherd pups must learn that the quickest way to switch off play is to become overly serious about what they are communicating. Early contact with other dogs in a fun, relaxed environment teaches them to loosen up, enjoy themselves and to develop a balanced attitude towards other dogs.

Controlled play

A good socialization class should not simply be a free-for-all, with all the puppies constantly playing together. It is vital that the play is controlled, and that the basics of training are taught, using only reward-based

methods. A good class should be able to show you how to build on the relationship you have with your puppy, and how to develop his natural instincts to your advantage. German Shepherds, like all herding/guarding types, are prone to wanting to round things up and/or bark at them! They quickly learn that barking in the car, or at people walking past the house, ensures that someone shouts, touches them or gets up to have a look, whereas playing quietly with a toy gets no attention at all.

German Shepherds are the rather serious, anxious-to-please types at puppy classes. They have an enormous desire to get things right, but are also incredibly sensitive to their owners' moods, which makes light-hearted, reward-based training even more imperative. Even slight disappointment from an owner can put a

HANDLING YOUR PUPPY

■ A good puppy class will also show owners how to prevent many basic behavioural problems occurring by being able to handle their puppy all over. This makes later veterinary examinations, treatment and grooming easy and stress-free. Of course, at this age all puppies are wriggly, and it is important that they learn to associate being groomed, handled, having their feet touched and their mouths looked at with pleasant things. A tasty treat or an exciting toy is essential to distract your puppy while you practise, allowing you to accustom your puppy to being inspected and touched.

■ Start this procedure of friendly and enjoyable handling from day one and you will be training your dog to cope with later experiences, such as nail clipping and teeth cleaning, without a struggle. Handling by lots of different people at this stage is also vital for German Shepherds. Capitalize on those cute floppy ears while they last and encourage children, men and women to handle your pup. For a breed that is traditionally suspicious of strangers, pleasurable touching and handling are vital if German Shepherds are to become friendly, loving family pets.

dog under pressure and many react by showing subtle signs of stress, such as panting or cringing. Some also react by becoming fearful of the environment – barking or lunging to keep everyone and everything else away from themselves and their beloved owner. This makes harsh training entirely inappropriate – the German Shepherd barking at other dogs in a more traditional class is not being 'naughty' or 'aggressive', but is reacting to stress, and should not be there.

Play biting

All puppies have needle-sharp teeth, and most of them appear to want to munch everything that moves. This is perfectly normal and is a vital stage of all dogs' development. Play biting, or puppy

biting, allows the puppy to discover information about his environment, and also about just how hard he can bite other puppies, and humans!

■ At this stage the puppy is learning a vital lesson – 'bite inhibition'. Watching puppies play together makes sense of this. Most puppies play by biting each other: one will bite the other's leg while another will grab an ear and hold on! All this is entirely friendly and playful – unless one of the pups bites the other a little too hard. If this bite hurts the puppy, he will give a really impressive yelp and will then refuse to play for the next few seconds. When the pups have regained their composure, play resumes, but the bites will now be significantly more gentle than before.

■ This is an ideal way to teach our puppies that we too feel pain. Humans need to communicate that they are hurt when their puppies mouth them, not that they are angry, which puppies regard as irrational aggression. Ideally, we can yelp loudly, or give a shout, then turn away as if to nurse our wounds. The puppy should look a little surprised when this first happens, but do not expect the biting to stop immediately. Gradually, over the next few weeks, the biting should become more and more gentle, until we yelp at the slightest pressure. Finally, we can show pain if a puppy even puts its teeth on us. The rule is then that humans are never to be bitten, even in play – we are too fragile.

■ Most puppies regard children as puppy-type playmates rather than humans to begin with, and adults may often need to help children out with this. Distracting the puppy with his toys and not letting either party become over-excited also helps. Time-outs, with the puppy confined in the crate or play pen for a short while, also allows things to calm down.

■ Learning bite inhibition is an essential lesson. Some individuals take longer than others to learn, but consistency is important. Most puppies lose their sharp puppy teeth at around eighteen to twenty weeks of age and need to have learned about the frailty of human skin before their adult teeth become established. Don't forget that puppy biting is not aggression – it is a learning process. A dog with good bite inhibition is a safe dog – make sure you teach it.

CHAPTER four

THE ADULT DOG

FOOD AND DIET

Commercially prepared foods are now the most common choice in feeding the pet dog. They are both convenient and cost-effective and there are now a multitude of foods to choose from. However, what looks delicious on an advertisement may not necessarily be suitable food for your pet dog.

German Shepherds can often be sensitive to diet, or to elements in their food. Although difficult to prove statistically, anecdotal evidence suggests that diet may have direct and indirect effects on dogs' behaviour and physiology, and an overactive dog, with little or no concentration span, may be helped by a change of diet.

All dogs, like all people, are different and as such have different requirements and different reactions to the various ingredients or elements in their diet. It is therefore always useful to look at this aspect of a dog's care if some behavioural difficulty is experienced.

Dog food is usually available as either moist food (in a can or chub), semi-moist, (usually packed in sealed plastic bags) or dry food (often in flake or pellet form in a plastic-lined sack). Of course, price and

TYPES OF DOG FOOD

Dog food is divided into two categories: complementary and complete. Most canned foods are described as being complementary. This means that they require an additional biscuit or mixer to add bulk to the diet and balance its components. Many of the dried foods, however, are complete foods. This means that they do not require any additional food to be added, and, in fact that adding anything to it may cause the balance of the food to be disturbed.

convenience will influence most people's choice, but it is vital to make sure that you understand the feeding instructions that come with each food.

Many behavioural and weight problems are caused by over-feeding, or by feeding incorrectly. Adding a can of food to an already complete dried food is only asking for trouble!

A nutritious, well-balanced diet is essential if your dog is to stay healthy.

Of course, it's not always possible to tell whether your dog is being adversely affected by the diet you are feeding. This is partly because it is often hard to know exactly what is in each food, and because if your dog looks well and healthy there may be no apparent reason to change.

Dogs also benefit from having their daily food allowance spread over the day, to prevent them from becoming overly hungry while waiting for their next feed. Many German Shepherd owners are now experiencing the benefits of feeding dogs two or more smaller meals per day rather than one large one, realising that the dogs are less likely to hang around the kitchen hoping for something to break their fast which would otherwise last twenty four hours. Tension levels and excitability may also be reduced in a dog that is not forced to wait all day before being fed. The digestive system is also less taxed by having to break down the contents of two smaller meals rather than one large one.

DIET AND BEHAVIOUR

Certain factors concerning your dog's health and behaviour may help you to look at whether his diet is suiting him. If your dog suffers regularly from one or more of the following, it might indicate that a change to his diet may help. Ask your vet for advice about changing your dog's diet and the options that are available to you.

- Frequent upset stomach.
- Wind.
- Allergic reactions to external factors such as fleas or grass
- Very smelly, very frequent, large motions.
- Under-weight despite eating substantial amounts of food
- Over-active/under-active
- Eating plants, grass, tissues or sticks
- Eating own faeces
- Rubbing, chewing or scratching at the base of the tail, feet or abdomen

EXERCISE

German Shepherd Dogs love physical exercise, and off-lead runs are essential if they are not to become bored or frustrated. The amount of exercise an adult German Shepherd will need depends on his lifestyle, breeding and fitness level, but a rough guideline is always as much as you can manage!

Of course, with off-lead exercise so important, training is paramount, as not everybody appreciates a large black and tan creature heading towards them at high speed. Many German Shepherds call up their herding instincts when out and about, and seem to take great delight in circling their owners, apparently trying to herd them in the required direction. Watching adult German Shepherds with other dogs they meet on a walk is also reminiscent of their herding abilities. Dogs that refuse to be 'penned' may well fall victim to the Shepherd's typical nip on the bottom, to keep them moving!

Of course, if not directed into more acceptable behaviour, such as chasing balls and toys when out for a walk, victims may otherwise be joggers or cyclists who may not appreciate the dog's likely peaceful intentions.

German Shepherds are also renowned for having to have the 'last word': a quick nip on the rear for

visitors to the house whom they believe have no right to be there. They are generally territorial types, taking their cues from those around them as to whether a stranger is friend or foe. However, while many will put up a brave front if guarding property, the majority prefer to send the unwary on their way back down the garden path from a rear position, not out in front! Early and continuing socialization will help prevent this happening to your visitors.

GROOMING

Grooming is minimal for short-coated dogs, although the long coats require daily brushing to ensure that the hair does not mat, particularly behind the ears and in the mass of hair that is the 'trousers'. However, it is important to brush or shine even the short-coated dogs with a hound glove or soft brush as frequently as possible to maintain good handling skills and co-operation.

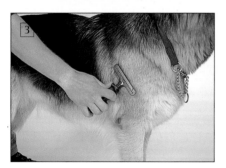

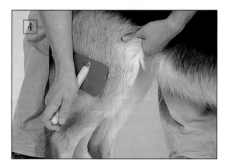

Grooming your German Shepherd need not take long if you follow this easy guide. Start by brushing the head and neck, especially behind the ears (1), and then comb the fur at the side of the head (2). Comb the chest (3) and brush through the longer fur on the 'trousers' (4) and the tail (5).

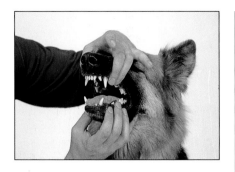 

Ears and teeth

Other aspects of general maintenance should include a regular inspection of the ears. Any brown or smelly discharge indicates an ear infection and should be dealt with promptly by your vet. Teeth should be checked, and brushed with a special dog toothpaste and soft brush at least once a day. Dogs build up tartar on their teeth in the same way as we do, and those that are on a soft diet of moist or semi-moist food are particularly susceptible. Tartar and eventual tooth decay result in bad breath as well as discomfort and eating problems.

Nail trimming

Many dogs do not particularly appreciate having their nails trimmed, and the art of easy nail clipping is always a good pair of quality nail clippers and to have accustomed the dog to lots of practice when young. Only the tiniest tip of each nail should be removed when cutting nails at home. The blood supply to the nail, the quick, runs through each claw and will bleed profusely if accidentally cut. Such an accident is also likely to make your dog wary of having his nails cut again. It is far better to trim the nails 'little and often' than take off too much at once and risk cutting the quick. The dew claw, sited on the inside of the dog's 'wrists' needs special attention if it is not to become curved and grow towards the skin. Trimming this claw needs a steady hand and a dog who is happy to be touched.

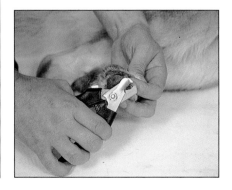

ONE TO ONE, OR ALL FOR ONE?

German Shepherds are active dogs when outdoors, although they can be calm and sensible when indoors with their family around them. A German Shepherd's paradise is to be constantly touching his owner in some way. They are known for being one-person dogs, but their devotion can border on obsession, making life difficult for all. While such loyalty can give confidence to those living alone, and makes them easily trained and biddable, it has many disadvantages if allowed to get out of hand. Behavioural problems tend to be centred around over-bonding to one person. Separation anxiety, nervousness and aggression to other people and dogs are

commonly associated with the German Shepherd. The irony is that whereas the image of the dog hunting down criminals or tackling intruders, reflects courage and tenacity, the majority of dogs without specialist training are rather cowardly, and take their cues and confidence from their owner, whom they hold in absolute awe and respect. This makes German Shepherds liable to bark and back away from a perceived 'threat'.

Sensitivity

Shepherds are sound-sensitive dogs, prone to fear-related problems around fireworks' night and thunderstorms. They are also highly sensitive to people's moods and emotions, and problems can arise if a German Shepherd decides to take action if he feels that his owner is threatened or anxious.

German Shepherds are also highly motivated by movement e.g. toys being thrown, or quarry disappearing into the undergrowth. This makes them easier to train using toys than many breeds, and a favourite game can keep a dog's attention focused for as long as you can play. However, it also makes them more likely to disappear after a moving lure than other types, and thus early training and socialization are vital.

TOYS AND PLAY

German Shepherds love toys, but many dog toys disintegrate as soon as they are chewed, whereas other lose their novelty value after a couple of days. Ideal toys are ones that are interactive, i.e. they maintain the dog's interest without having to have a human on the other end. German Shepherds are prone to separation problems and chewing can help to relieve the boredom or frustration of social isolation. Leaving safe toys for your dog to play with while you are out is a wise precaution.

Hollow sterilized bones and hollow rubber toys are ideal, especially if the owner has the foresight to stuff them full of interesting food morsels, just out of tongue's reach. These can provide hours of entertainment, particularly while human company is not available.

WARNING

Throwing sticks for any dog when outside is not a good idea. Vets have to treat far too many emergency cases every year after sticks have become impaled in dogs' mouths or throats. Wood can also splinter and cause damage to the gut lining. Many dogs also choke on balls which are too small for them and get stuck in their throats, and some of the larger pieces of flat raw hide chews can also become lodged at the back of the throat, causing suffocation. Choose your dog's toys with care.

FAMILY PLANNING

Unless you wish to breed from your dog, it is sensible to have dogs castrated and bitches spayed. This saves a great amount of time chasing your male after he has escaped in search of bitches from your supposedly impenetrable garden, and warding off amorous males from your driveway to protect your bitch from their advances when in season.

Many cross-breeds seem to have a smattering of German Shepherd-type input. With so many dogs needing homes it is inexcusable to allow either a dog or a bitch to produce an unwanted litter. Talk to your vet about neutering.

Sexual maturity

German Shepherds may not be fully socially mature until three years old, but sexual maturity tends to influence males' behaviour from around seven months.

At this time, many need a second bout of concentrated socialization, particularly with other dogs, as the 'teenage stage' can transform an adorable puppy into a hooligan in a matter of weeks! Once again, they may need a refresher course in the body language of other dogs.

They seem surprised that not all dogs want to play in the same rough way as them, and many get themselves into trouble with adult males of other breeds which may not appreciate being romped so energetically. One or two bad experiences at this stage often puts dogs and owners off mixing freely with other dogs in the park, and this is usually the start of an ongoing and ever-increasing problem with other dogs. Castration at this stage can help, but there is no substitute for continuing to socialize your German Shepherd with as many other dogs and people as possible right through his adolescence.

Rehoming a dog

Sadly, there are all too many German Shepherds awaiting new homes in rescue centres. Many are also cared for by breed rescue societies which try to place dogs with new families if they can no longer live with their original owners. Although many are simply the innocent victims of financial problems, marriage break-ups and house repossessions, a typical dog languishing in a rescue centre kennel is more than likely to be around eleven to eighteen months old, and male.

House rules

It is not impossible to transform a rescue dog from an anxious, or over-excitable dog into a sensible companion, but it does take hard work and commitment. Generally speaking, house rules need to be in place from day one. No matter how sorry you feel for your dog's past, what he needs now is security.

Dogs thrive on routines that are set by the owner. They like to know where they stand in the family: which resources are theirs, what they cannot touch. Many will quickly establish themselves as dictator of your day and, more importantly, your attention, if they

are not guided from the beginning. All dogs that are taken into a new home tend to behave absolutely beautifully for the first few days or couple of weeks. This is known as the 'honeymoon period' by behaviour counsellors! It is during this time that the dog is watching to see what goes on in the household on

TAKING ON A REHOUSED DOG

This is often a good option for people who do not wish to have to start from scratch with a new puppy, and who want to give a loving home to a dog that has fallen on hard times. However, it is wise to realise from the outset that only a lucky minority of people taking on a rescue dog will find it is house-trained, sociable with people and other animals and the perfect companion. More often than not, rescue dogs come with their own idiosyncrasies, imperfections and, on occasions, behaviour problems which need time, experience, and patience to solve.

few days, or was always granted in his previous home, or as any over-bonding occurs with new owners. For example, many new owners take time off work to settle their new dog in at home. The dog follows them from room to room for two weeks, and then is left utterly abandoned and isolated when the owner returns to work. Above all, the message has to be: start as you mean to go on.

Boarding kennels

German Shepherds tend to adapt quite well to time spent in boarding kennels, unless they are so over-bonded to their owners that they cannot bear to be parted from them.

■ Many people find a good kennel by word of mouth, and recommendation from someone who has used the kennel and been pleased with the service is the ideal way to find out about the best in your area. However, it is always worth the effort to inspect the kennels yourself, to put your mind at rest about the kind of accommodation and care your dog will receive when you are away.

■ Make the effort to chat with the staff. Do they seem knowledgeable and helpful? Are they prepared to try to fit in with your dog's usual routine as far as possible? Many dogs that are used to having two meals a day rather than just one, eat better if they are allowed to stick to this routine.

a day-to-day basis. Dogs watch people and their interactions with each other.

During this time, most rescue dogs are slightly subdued, working on the principle that until they feel more secure in their new environment it is better to keep their heads down and work out the system! At some stage the dog is going to begin to feel more secure, and this is when problems are more likely to occur. This is not necessarily a canine takeover bid, but merely a chance to raise objections over the removal of resources that the dog has been granted over the first

■ The biggest favour you can do your dog, and the kennel owners, is to make sure that your dog is not going to be desperately unhappy because he has never experienced kennel life before.

■ Ideally, it is a good idea to get your dog used to boarding by leaving him at the kennels you have chosen for a day, and then possibly a night as well, when he is as young as possible. Even if your dog is already adult, allowing him to gradually cope with the strange sounds and smells of the kennels by spending small amounts of time there is much better than throwing him in at the deep end – leaving him there for the first time ever for two solid weeks, and expecting him not to bark himself hoarse!

■ Of course, if you live with a dog that won't even let you go to the bathroom without wanting to come with you, then leaving him in kennels for any length of time is going to be a big shock. If your dog is still quite young, it is worth trying to cool your relationship with him gradually and this is best done with the help of a behaviour counsellor.

Home sitters

An alternative option for those German Shepherd owners who do not wish to kennel their dog is the rapidly expanding industry of home sitters. There are now many specialist and reputable agencies which organise an experienced and animal-loving person to look after your pets in the comfort of your own home while you are away on holiday, or to visit your dog on a number of occasions throughout the day, if you are not actually staying away from home but go to work. This service can be a distinct advantage if you have a number of pets at home, which all have different requirements regarding feeding and exercising etc.

SEPARATION PROBLEMS

Some German Shepherds tend to develop separation problems as they become older. It is quite common for those dogs that have previously been adaptable to become constant companions of their beloved owners in their twilight years, shadowing them constantly and coming to depend on them totally. Separation anxiety may be exacerbated by failing eyesight, or dwindling hearing, resulting in a continual need for reassurance, and often physical contact, from their owners. Dogs separated from their owners may become extremely distressed, and may howl or lose toilet control. In this situation it is sometimes better to look at making your faithful companion's existence as happy as possible, rather than attempting to cure the problem outright. After many years as adoring pets, our loyalty to our dogs in their old age counts for a lot.

SHOWING

ENTERING A DOG SHOW

When buying a dog most people look for a companion and family pet. However, for many of us owning a dog brings a degree of pride of ownership and we begin to wonder how well our pet compares with others of the same breed. Many people go to training classes to educate their dog and to ensure that it is properly trained, and there they are bound to meet others who have made a

SHOWS IN YOUR AREA

The breeder from whom you purchased your puppy should be able to give you some indication of the general shows that are held in your area. However, if you are going to take showing seriously you should regularly take one of the weekly dog newspapers that print advertisements for shows and a list of those for which the entries are closing that particular week. They also provide you with a great deal of information about the show scene and you will find a small section devoted to your breed under the breed notes. The canine press also publish reports of most dog shows, which are written by the judges.

hobby of showing their dog. For most people, showing is just that – an enjoyable hobby – but for many others it can become a consuming passion, even perhaps an obsession. Whatever the strength of your commitment, to get the best out of your dog is time consuming.

Learning about showing

If you are interested in showing your dog, your first step should be to join a breed club. Through its members, its shows, its training days and newsletters, you will quickly pick up the basic requirements of presenting your German Shepherd to his best advantage. For details of your nearest breed club, contact the Kennel Club (see page 144).

The Kennel Club is the ruling body for the world of British dog shows, working trials, field trials, obedience and agility trials. It also runs Cruft's dog show in addition to providing all the rules and regulations that are needed to ensure that showing your dog is as fair as possible

Ulk von Arlett, the winner of the 1995 Bundessieger-Zuchtschau in Hamburg.

Types of dog show

There are several types of show in the same way that there are several leagues in the world of soccer.

■ **Championship Shows** are the most prestigious as there are Challenge Certificates available for each breed. The number of Challenge Certificates that are available in any one year is worked out by using a formula that takes into account the number of dogs in that breed being shown. The larger the number of dogs, the more Challenge Certificates are available and vice versa.

However, the number awarded com-pared to the number of dogs being shown in the breed is really quite small, and therefore these certificates are important because if a dog can win three of them under different judges he is entitled to be called a champion. Naturally, there is fierce competition at this level.

Championship shows are either general championship shows where most or many of the breeds are scheduled, or breed championship shows, which are, of course, restricted to one breed only.

You must learn to 'stand' your dog, as shown at the prestigious Sieger show.

■ **Open Shows** are the next level, and many hundreds of these are held each year. These are the shows where you will meet many friends and where your dog will cut his showing teeth. Competition is sometimes quite strong because many breeders and exhibitors use open shows to bring out their young dogs for practice, and sometimes to take their older ones just for a day out even though they have been very successful at championship show level.

■ **Other shows** include Limited Shows, which are restricted to members of a particular society, Sanction Shows, Primary Shows, Matches and Exemption Shows.

Attending a show

Whichever sort of show you attend, the pattern is the same.

1 Firstly, you will need to obtain a schedule and entry form from the Secretary. Most Secretaries prefer you to write in enclosing a stamped addressed envelope, but nowadays many are happy to send you a schedule on receipt of a telephone request. Particularly with the big shows, don't be surprised if you find yourself speaking to an answering machine; the number of enquiries that are received by a Show Secretary as the entries closing date approaches can be many hundreds a day.

2 Having got your schedule, you will need to select the classes that you wish to enter and then complete the entry

You can start off by showing your dog at an exemption show. These shows are enjoyable for both the owner and dog.

form, giving all the details requested.

3 Of course, your dog will need to be transferred to your name at the Kennel Club, but if the paperwork has not come through you may enter the dog's name with 'TAF' in brackets afterwards. This means 'transfer applied for'. If, for any reason, your dog's name has not yet been accepted by the Kennel Club, you can enter it 'NAF', meaning 'name applied for'.

4 This system is in use for all shows other than primary shows, matches and exemption shows. Entries must be

made in advance – sometimes more than two months ahead of the show date. This is to allow the entries to be counted so that sufficient benches and tenting can be arranged and the show catalogues printed, including all the details that you set out on the entry form.

Classes

You will see from the schedule that the breed or variety is divided into various classes. Some have obvious names such as 'Puppy', which is for dog up to one year old, and 'Junior', which is for dogs up to eighteen months of age, and 'Open', which means that any dog can enter.

The judge will want to watch the way your dog moves in the show ring.

THE THRILL OF WINNING

By this time, you will have realised that showing dogs can be an expensive hobby for there is certainly little in the way of prize money to be won. However, everyone who is involved does it for fun and the thrill of winning and, of course, those green Challenge Certificates which allow us to put the title 'Champion' before the name of our dog.

However, the intermediate classes may cause you some confusion. You will find definitions of these classes in the schedule, and, in effect, they mean that if your dog has had a certain amount of wins, he stops being eligible for that particular class. Eligibility is different for

different shows, and therefore you do need to check the schedule to make sure that you have entered in the correct class.

Benching

Larger shows, especially championship shows, are usually benched with the dogs on special trestles which are partitioned off to allow room for each dog to lie down quietly. These days, most smaller shows are not benched and, although benching is expensive, there is no doubt that having to look after your dogs throughout the day and keep them with you wherever you go can sometimes be a bit of a chore. However, most novices have only one dog and therefore it is not really a problem.

Judging

Judges are selected by the show society for their experience and knowledge of the breed, or breeds, that they are judging. Some judges are very good and some, of course, are not so good, although those that judge badly usually do so as a result of incompetence rather than dishonesty!

Successful showing

The secret of success is consistency: no dog ever wins under every judge and few dogs ever lose under every judge. How good your dog is depends largely on how consistent you are. If you usually win or are placed in the top three, then you have almost certainly got a very good dog. If

RINGCRAFT

When the time comes for you to enter your class, you should go into the ring and the steward will tell you where to stand. It is very sensible to spend some time watching the other exhibitors so that you have some idea of the procedure when you approach the judge.

■ The judge will usually ask you to come forward and 'stand' your dog. Watch other exhibitors to see how this is done – don't stand at the front of the line in your first class at your first show.

■ The judge will then examine the dog from a distance, look at him probably from the front and the back, approach the dog and check his eyes, teeth, structure and musculature, and the overall conformation.

■ The judge will then ask you to move the dog. Different judges require dogs to move in different ways so watch carefully and listen to the instructions. After a final look, the judge will move on to the next dog.

you are usually not considered or left down at the bottom of the line, then, after a period of time, you will have to accept that your dog is not quite as good an example of the breed as you thought he was or would like him to be. The important thing to remember is that whatever the results of the competition you will always take the best dog home – and that's your dog!

PART THREE

HEALTHCARE

In this section on healthcare, there is expert practical advice on keeping your dog healthy and preventing many common health problems, together with information on canine illnesses and diseases and the special health problems that may affect the breed, especially inherited ones. If you are considering breeding from your dog, you will find everything that you need to know about mating, whelping and weaning the puppies. Essential first-aid techniques for use in accidents and emergencies are also featured.

HEALTH MAINTENANCE

Throughout the health section of this book, where comments relate equally to the dog or the bitch, we have used the term 'he' to avoid the repeated, clumsy use of 'he or she'. Your German Shepherd is definitely not an 'it'.

SIGNS OF A HEALTHY DOG

■ Appearance and behaviour
In general, a healthy dog looks healthy. He wants to play with you, as games are a very important part of a dog's life. He is always ready for his walk.

■ Eyes
His eyes are bright and alert, and, apart from the small amount of 'sleep' in the inner corners, there is no discharge. His nose is usually cold and wet with no discharge, although a little clear fluid can be normal.

■ Ears
His ears are also alert and very responsive to sounds around him. In the German Shepherd, ears are usually held erect. The inside of his ear flap is pale pink in appearance and silky in texture. No wax will be visible and there will be no unpleasant smell. He will not scratch his ears much, or shake his head excessively.

■ Coat
A healthy German Shepherd Dog's coat, whether of the short- or long-haired variety, will be glossy and feel pleasant to the touch. He will not scratch excessively and scurf will be not be present. His coat will smell 'doggy' but not unpleasant, and he will probably shed hairs (moult) continuously, to some degree, especially if he lives indoors with the family.

■ Teeth
The teeth of a healthy dog should be white and smooth. If they are yellow and dull, there may be plaque or tartar formation.

■ Claws
A dog's claws should not be broken or too long. Each one has a short non-sensitive tip, as in our nails. The claw should end at the ground, level with the pad. Dogs will not pay much attention to their feet, apart from normal washing, but excessive licking can indicate disease. German Shepherds have five toes on the front feet, with one in our 'thumb' position, called the dew claw, and four on the hind feet. If a puppy is born with a dew claw on a hind foot, it is usually removed at between three and five days of age as they become pendulous and are often injured when the dog becomes an adult.

■ Stools
A healthy dog will pass stools between once and six times a day, depending on diet, temperament, breed and opportunity.

■ Urination
A male dog will urinate numerous times on a walk as this is territorial behaviour. Bitches usually urinate less often.

■ Weight
A healthy dog will look in good bodily condition for his size – not too fat and not too thin. Sixty per cent of dogs nowadays are overweight, so take care to balance the diet with the right amount of exercise.

■ Feeding
A dog will usually be ready for his meal and, once adult, he should be fed regularly at the

POINTS OF THE DOG

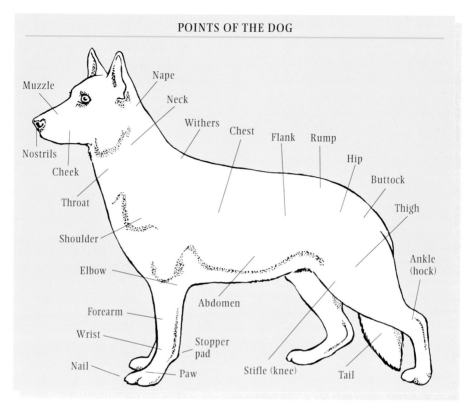

Muzzle

Nape

Neck

Nostrils

Withers

Chest

Flank

Rump

Hip

Buttock

Cheek

Thigh

Throat

Shoulder

Ankle
(hock)

Elbow

Abdomen

Forearm

Wrist

Stopper
pad

Nail

Paw

Stifle (knee)

Tail

same time each day. Most dogs require one meal a day, but some healthy dogs seem to need two meals daily just to maintain a normal weight. These are the very active dogs who tend to 'burn off' more calories.

DIET

■ Puppies

It is essential to feed a puppy the correct diet in order to allow him to achieve his full potential during the growing phase. In a German Shepherd, this is up to eighteen months to two years of age. Many home-made diets are deficient in various ingredients just because owners do not fully appreciate

the balance that is required. It is far better to rely on one of the correctly formulated and prepared commercial diets, which will contain the correct amounts and proportions of essential nutrients such as protein, carbohydrates, fats, roughage, minerals such as calcium and phosphorus, and essential vitamins.

■ Complete dried diets

Modern thinking is that the complete dried, extruded diets that are now available have so many advantages that the new puppy could be put on to a 'growth' formula diet of this type from as early as four weeks of age. Crunchy diets have advantages in dental care also.

■ **Canned and semi-moist diets**

There are some excellent canned and semi-moist diets available, too. However, care should be taken to check whether these are complete diets, or complementary foods which require the addition of biscuits and other ingredients. Of course, if you really know about nutrition and diets, it is possible to formulate a home-prepared diet from fresh ingredients.

■ **Feeding puppies**

A puppy should be fed four times a day until he is three months old, and, with a complete dried food, this can be left down so that he can help himself to food whenever he feels

CARE OF THE OLDER DOG

Provided that he has been well cared for throughout his life, there may be no need to treat the older German Shepherd Dog any differently as old age approaches. However, here is some general advice on caring for the older dog.

Diet and feeding

Your dog's diet should be chosen carefully to:
■ Improve existing problems.
■ Slow or prevent the development of disease.
■ Enable the dog to maintain his ideal body weight.
■ Be highly palatable and digestible.
■ Contain an increased amount of fatty acids, vitamins (especially A, B and E) and certain minerals, notably zinc.
■ Contain reduced amounts of protein, phosphorus and sodium.

Fitness and exercise

A healthy dog should hardly need to reduce his exercise until he is over ten years old. There should be no sudden change in routine; a sudden increase in exercise is as wrong as a sudden drop. Let the dog let you know when he has had enough. If he lags behind, has difficulty in walking or breathing or getting to his feet after a long walk, then it is time to consider a health check. As dogs age, they need a good diet, company, comfort and sometimes a change of scenery to add interest to their lives.

Avoiding obesity

■ As the body ages, all body systems age with it. The heart and circulation, lungs, muscles and joints are not as efficient as they once were. These should all be able to support and transport a dog of the correct weight but may fail if the dog is grossly overweight.
■ A dog of normal weight will approach old age with a greater likelihood of reaching it. It is wise to diet your dog at this stage if you have let his weight increase. Food intake can be increased almost to normal when the weight loss has been achieved.
■ Reduce the calorie intake to about sixty per cent of your dog's normal intake, to encourage the conversion of body fat back into energy. Feed a high-fibre diet so that the dog does not feel hungry. Maintenance levels of essential nutrients, such as protein, vitamins and minerals, must be provided so that deficiencies do not occur.
■ Your veterinary surgeon will be able to supply or advise on the choice of several prescription low-calorie diets which are available in both dried and canned form, or he will instruct you on how to mix your own.

hungry. The exact amount of food will depend on his age and the type of food offered. If instructions are not included on the packet, you should consult your vet.

At three months of age, he should be fed three times daily, but each meal should be larger. By six months of age, he could be down to two larger meals a day – still of a puppy or growth-formula food. He should remain on this type of food until he is between twelve and eighteen months old, and then change to an adult maintenance version.

■ **Adult dogs**

Adult dogs can be fed on any one of the excellent range of quality dog foods now available. Your vet is the best person to advise you as to the best diet for your German Shepherd, and this advice will vary depending on his age, daily amount of exercise and general condition.

■ **Elderly dogs**

From the age of nine or ten years onwards, your German Shepherd may benefit from changing to a diet that is specially formulated for the older dog, as he will have differing requirements as his body organs age a little. Your vet is the best person with whom to discuss this, as he will be able to assess your dog's general condition and requirements.

EXERCISE

Exercising a puppy

■ **Pre-vaccination exercise**

As a puppy, your German Shepherd should not be given too much exercise relative to his size. At the age at which you acquire him, usually between six and eight weeks, he will need gentle, frequent forays into your garden, or other people's gardens provided they are secure, excape-proof and not open to stray dogs. He can and should meet other vaccinated, reliable dogs or puppies and play with them. He will also enjoy energetic games with you, but remember that in any tug-of-war type of contest you should win!

Although you should take your puppy out with you to accustom him to the sights and sounds of normal life, at this stage you should not put him down on the ground in public places until the vaccination course is completed, because of the risk of infection.

■ **Exercise after vaccination**

About a week after his second vaccination, you will be able to take your puppy out for walks, but remember that at this stage he is equivalent to a toddler. His bones have not calcified, his joints are still developing, and too much strenuous exercise can affect his normal development. This applies especially to large breeds with rapid growth, such as German Shepherds, which at this stage may be gaining up to 2 kg (3^1/$_2$lb) a week.

Perhaps three walks daily, of about half an hour each, are ample by about four months of age, rising to a total of two to three hours by the time he reaches six months. At this stage, as his bones and joints develop, he could then be taken for more vigorous runs in the park or country. However, he should not be involved in really tiring exercise until he is at least nine months to a year old, by which time his joints have almost fully matured and his bones are fully calcified.

Exercising an adult dog

■ **Daily exercise**

As an adult dog, the German Shepherd's exercise tolerance will be almost limitless, certainly better than most of ours! It is essential that such a lively, active, intelligent breed has an adequate amount of exercise daily – it is not really sufficient to provide exercise just at weekends. A daily quota of one to two hours of interesting, energetic exercise is essential. As the German Shepherd usually bonds very closely to his owner, often one person in a couple in particular, he will stay close to you on a walk, wandering off from time to time, and coming back frequently to check that you are still around.

■ **Games during exercise**

During exercise, German Shepherds enjoy games, such as retrieving and finding hidden objects, so try to exercise your dog's brain as well as his body.

DAILY CARE

There are several things that you should be doing on a daily basis for your dog in order to keep him healthy and in first-class condition.

■ **Grooming**

All dogs benefit from a daily grooming session. Use a stiff brush or comb obtained from your vet or pet shop, and make sure you specify that it is for a German Shepherd Dog as brushes vary a great deal. Comb or brush in the direction of the lie of the hair. Hair is constantly growing and being shed, especially in dogs that live indoors with us, as their bodies become confused as to which season it is in a uniformly warm house. Brushing removes dead hair and scurf, and stimulates the sebaceous glands to produce the natural oils that keep the coat glossy.

■ **Bathing**

Dogs should not require frequent baths, but they can benefit from a periodic shampoo using a specially formulated dog shampoo with a conditioner included.

■ **Feeding**

Dogs do not benefit from a frequently changed diet. Their digestive systems seem to grow accustomed to a regular diet; dogs do not worry if they have the same food to eat every day – that is a human trait – so establish a complete nutritious diet that your dog enjoys and then stick to it. German Shepherds are prone to digestive problems, and a regular established daily diet is one way of minimizing these.

The day's food should be given at a regular time each day. Usually the adult dog will have one meal a day, either at breakfast-time or tea-time. Both feeding times are equally acceptable but, ideally, hard exercise should not be given within an hour of a full meal. It is better to take your dog for a long walk and then feed him on your return. Some dogs seem to prefer two smaller meals a day, and this is perfectly acceptable, provided that the total amount of food given is not excessive.

■ **Water**

Your German Shepherd should have a full bowl of clean, fresh water, changed once or twice a day, and this should be permanently available. This is particularly important if he is on a complete dried food type of diet.

■ **Toileting**

Your dog should be let out into the garden first thing in the morning to toilet. This can be taught quite easily on command and in a specified area of the garden. You should not take the dog out for a walk to toilet, unless you just do not have a garden or the space at home. The mess should be on your property and then picked up and flushed down the toilet daily. Other people, children in particular, should not have to put up with our dogs' mess.

Throughout the day, your dog should have

access to a toileting area every few hours, and always last thing at night before you all go to bed. Dogs will usually want to, and can be conditioned to, defecate immediately after a meal, so this should be encouraged.

■ Company

German Shepherds are very sociable dogs and bond to you strongly. There is no point having one unless you intend to be with him most of the time. Obviously, a well-trained and socialized adult should be capable of being left for one to three hours at a time, but puppies need constant attention if they are to grow up well balanced. Games, as mentioned before, are an essential daily pastime.

■ Dental care

Some complete diets are very crunchy, and by mimicking the wild dog's (e.g. foxes, wolves) diet of a whole rabbit (bones, fur etc.), for instance, these will keep your dog's teeth relatively free of plaque and tartar. However, a daily teeth inspection is sensible. Lift the lips and look at not just the front incisor and

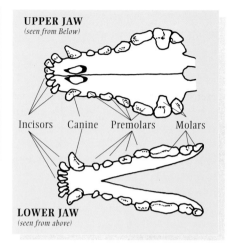

UPPER JAW
(seen from Below)

Incisors   Canine   Premolars   Molars

LOWER JAW
(seen from above)

canine teeth but also the back premolars and molars. They should be a healthy, shiny white like ours and the gums pink and healthy.

If not, or if your dog is fed a soft, canned or fresh meat diet, daily brushing, using a toothbrush and enzyme toothpaste, is advisable. Hide chew sticks help clean teeth, as do root vegetables such as carrots, and many

VACCINATIONS

Vaccination is the administration of a modified live, or killed form of, infection, which does not cause illness in the dog, but instead stimulates the formation of antibodies against the disease itself. There are four major diseases against which all dogs should be vaccinated. These are:

■ Canine distemper (also called hard pad)
■ Infectious canine hepatitis
■ Leptospirosis
■ Canine parvovirus

Many vaccination courses now include a component against parainfluenza virus, one of the causes of kennel cough, that scourge

of boarding and breeding kennels. A separate vaccine against bordetella, another cause of kennel cough, can be given in droplet form down the nose prior to your dog entering boarding kennels. All these diseases are described in Chapter Seven.

■ Vaccinating puppies

In the puppy, vaccination should start at eight to ten weeks of age, and consists of a course of two injections, two to four weeks apart. It is recommended that adult dogs have an annual check-up and booster inoculation from the vet.

vets recommend a large raw marrow bone. However, occasionally these can cause teeth to break so exercise caution. Various manufacturers have brought out tasty, chewy food items that benefit teeth, and your vet will be able to recommend a suitable one.

Puppies are born with, or acquire shortly after birth, a full set of temporary teeth. These start to be shed at about sixteen weeks of age with the central incisors, and the transition from temporary to permanent teeth should be complete by the time they are six months old. If extra teeth seem to be present, or if teeth seem out of position at this age, it is wise to see your vet.

■ **General inspection**

A full inspection by you is not necessary on a daily basis, unless you notice something different about your dog. However, it is as well to cast your eyes over him to ensure that his coat and skin are in good order, his eyes are bright, his ears are clean, and he is not lame Check that he has eaten his food, and that his stools and urine look normal.

PERIODIC HEALTH CARE

Worming

■ **Roundworms (Toxocara)**

All puppies should be wormed fortnightly from two weeks to three months of age, and then monthly up to six months of age. Thereafter in a male or neutered female German Shepherd, you should worm your dog twice yearly. Bitches used for breeding have special roundworming requirements and these are covered in Chapter Eight. There is evidence that entire females undergoing false (pseudo) pregnancies have roundworm larvae migrating in their tissues, so they should be wormed at this time.

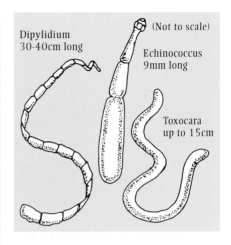

Dipylidium
30-40cm long

(Not to scale)

Echinococcus
9mm long

Toxocara
up to 15cm

■ **Tapeworms (Dipylidium and Echinococcus)**

These need intermediate hosts (fleas and usually sheep offal respectively) to complete their life cycle, so prevention of contact with these is advisable. As a precaution, most vets recommend tapeworming adult dogs twice a year. There are very effective, safe combined round and tape worm treatments available now from your vet.

SPECIAL HEALTH PROBLEMS

The German Shepherd Dog is usually a fit, friendly and interesting companion. However, there are some health problems that are known to occur in this breed particularly. A few of the more common problems are detailed below.

■ **Hip dysplasia**

This is by far the most common inherited disease of the German Shepherd Dog and is dealt with more fully in Chapter Seven. It is a malformation of one or both hip joints, and may not be detectable until the dog is a young adult or even older. Stiffness on rising, an odd bunny-hopping gait, or lameness are the usual signs. You can reduce the chances of your dog being affected by checking the hip scores of the puppy's parents, and by keeping exercise to a gentle level until your dog is at least six months old.

■ **OCD, or osteochondritis dissicans**

This is a disease of the joints, causing cartilage not to join on to the growing bone correctly. It can affect any joint, but usually it is the shoulder or elbow joints that are involved. Reduce the chances of your dog being affected by keeping exercise to a gentle level until your dog is at least six months old.

■ **Epilepsy**

This condition is seen more often in the German Shepherd than in many other breeds. The dog has a sudden, unexpected fit or convulsion, which lasts for about two minutes. Recovery is fairly quick, although the dog may be dull and look confused for a few hours. Treatment is usually necessary and successful as far as control of epilepsy is concerned.

■ **CDRM, or chronic degenerative radiculo myelopathy**

This is a gradually progressive paralysis of the hind legs, which usually begins in late middle age. The cause is not known and, as most dogs have finished breeding when they show the symptoms, it is difficult to avoid buying a puppy from an affected parent. Ask whether the line has any history of the disease.

■ **Anal furunculosis**

This is a deep penetrating infection of the tissues around the anus. It is thought to be more common in the German Shepherd due to the way in which the bushy tail is carried, curving down low over the anus. This prevents fuller ventilation of the area.

■ **Haemophilia A**

This is a failure of certain clotting mechanisms which will lead to virtually

PET HEALTH INSURANCE AND VETS' FEES

By choosing a puppy wisely, and then ensuring that your dog is fit and of the right weight, occupied both mentally and physically, protected against disease by vaccination, and fed correctly, you should be able to minimize any vets' bills. However, the unexpected may well happen, and accidents and injuries do occur. Dogs can also develop life-long allergies or long-term illnesses, such as diabetes. To protect you against these unexpected eventualities, pet health insurance is available and is recommended by the vast majority of veterinarians. It is important to take out a policy that will suit you and your German Shepherd Dog, so it is wise to ask your veterinary surgeon for his recommendation.

uncontrollable haemorrhage. Although still uncommon, it is seen in the German Shepherd more than in most other breeds.

■ **von Willebrand's disease**

This is an inherited disease of another blood component, the platelets, and causes haemorrhage. The German Shepherd Dog and Doberman seem to head the list.

■ **Pancreatic hypoplasia**

This is a more common condition, leading to a thin, hungry dog with an excessive appetite. The food cannot be digested and the faeces are bulky and often fatty in appearance.

Note: You can reduce the chances of your new dog having these problems by asking the right questions about his ancestry before you purchase him.

CHAPTER SEVEN

DISEASES AND ILLNESSES

RESPIRATORY DISEASES

■ Rhinitis

This infection of the nose, which is caused by viruses, bacteria or fungi, is fairly common in the German Shepherd Dog. It may also be part of a disease such as distemper or kennel cough. Sneezing or a clear or coloured discharge are the usual signs.

Another cause, due to the dog's habit of sniffing, is a grass seed or other foreign object inhaled through the nostrils. The dog starts to sneeze violently, often after a walk through long grass.

■ Tumours of the nose

Tumours of the nose are quite common in the German Shepherd Dog. The first sign is often haemorrhage from one nostril. X-rays reveal a mass in the nasal chamber.

■ Laryngeal paralysis

This is a disease that affects old dogs, and it does occur in the German Shepherd Dog. The vocal cords become paralysed, obstruct the airway and vibrate on inspiration, causing a snoring noise.

Diseases producing a cough

A cough is a reflex which clears foreign matter from the bronchi, trachea and larynx. Severe inflammation of these structures will also stimulate the cough reflex.

■ Laryngitis, tracheitis and bronchitis

Inflammation of the larynx, trachea and bronchi can be caused by infection, such as kennel cough or canine distemper, by irritant fumes or by foreign material. Usually, all three parts of the airway are affected at the same time.

Bronchitis is a major problem in the older dog caused by a persistent infection or irritation, producing irreversible changes in the bronchi. A cough develops and increases until the dog seems to cough almost constantly.

Diseases producing laboured breathing

Laboured breathing is normally caused by those diseases that occupy space within the chest, and reduce the lung tissue available for oxygenation of the blood. An X-ray produces an accurate diagnosis.

■ Pneumonia

This is an infection of the lungs. Although it is uncommon in the German Shepherd Dog, it

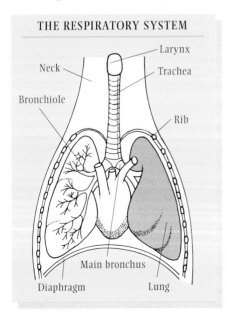

THE RESPIRATORY SYSTEM

- Larynx
- Neck
- Trachea
- Bronchiole
- Rib
- Main bronchus
- Diaphragm
- Lung

INFECTIOUS DISEASES

■ **Distemper (hardpad)**

This is a frequently fatal virus disease, which usually affects dogs under one year of age. Affected dogs cough and have a discharge from the eyes and nose. Pneumonia often develops, and vomiting and diarrhoea usually follow. If the dog lives, nervous symptoms, such as fits, paralysis or chorea (a type of regular twitch), are likely. The pads of the feet become thickened and hard – hence the other name for the disease, hard pad.

Treatment by antibiotics sometimes helps, but the only real answer is prevention by vaccination as a puppy, and annual boosters.

■ **Infectious canine hepatitis**

This affects the liver. In severe cases, the first sign may be that the dog goes completely off his food, becomes very depressed and collapses. Some affected dogs die suddenly. Recovery is unlikely from this severe form of the disease. Prevention by vaccination is essential.

■ **Leptospirosis**

Two separate diseases affect dogs. Both, in addition to causing severe and often fatal disease in the dog, are infectious to humans.

■ **Leptospira canicola** causes acute kidney disease.

■ **Leptospira icterohaemorrhagiae** causes an acute infection of the liver, often leading to jaundice.

Treatment of both is often unsuccessful, and prevention by vaccination is essential.

■ **Canine parvovirus**

This affects the bowels, causing a sudden onset of vomiting and diarrhoea, often with blood, and severe depression. As death is usually due to dehydration, prompt replacement of the fluid and electrolyte loss is essential. In addition, antibiotics are usually given to prevent secondary bacterial infection. Prevention by vaccination is essential.

■ **Kennel cough**

This is a highly infectious cough occurring mainly in kennelled dogs. There are two main causes: bordetella, a bacterial infection; and parainfluenza virus, both of which affect the trachea and lungs. Occasionally, a purulent discharge from the nose and eyes may develop. Antibiotics and rest are usually prescribed by the vet. Prevention of both by vaccination is recommended.

can occur, caused by viruses, bacteria, fungi or foreign material.

■ **Chest tumours**

These can cause respiratory problems by occupying lung space and by causing the accumulation of fluid within the chest.

Accidents

Respiratory failure commonly follows many

accidents. Several types of injury may be seen, as listed below:

■ **Haemorrhage into the lung**

Rupture of a blood vessel in the lung will release blood which fills the air sacs.

■ **Ruptured diaphragm**

This allows abdominal organs, such as the liver, spleen or stomach, to move forward into the chest cavity.

Note: see pages 127-138.

HEART AND CIRCULATION DISEASES

Heart attack

In the human sense, this is uncommon in dogs. Collapse or fainting may occur due to inadequate cardiac function.

Heart murmurs

■ **Acquired disease** may result from wear and tear or inflammation of the heart valves, problems of rhythm and rate, or disease of the heart muscle. Signs of disease may include weakness, lethargy, panting, coughing, abdominal distension, collapse and weight loss.

SIGNS OF HEART FAILURE

These may include the following:
■ Exercise intolerance
■ Lethargy
■ Panting and/or cough
■ Enlargement of the abdomen due to fluid accumulation
■ Poor digestion and weight loss
Veterinary investigation involves thorough examination, possibly X-rays of the chest, ECG and, in some cases, ultrasound scanning

■ **Congenital heart disease** is usually due to valve defects or a hole in the heart. Signs of

THE CIRCULATORY SYSTEM

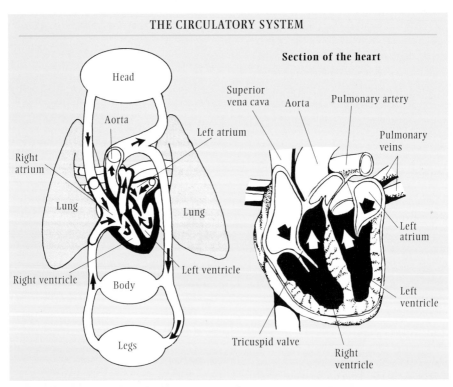

Section of the heart

Head

Aorta

Right atrium

Lung

Lung

Right ventricle

Body

Left ventricle

Legs

Superior vena cava

Aorta

Pulmonary artery

Left atrium

Pulmonary veins

Left atrium

Left ventricle

Tricuspid valve

Right ventricle

disease may include the sudden death of a puppy, or weakness and failure to thrive or grow at a normal rate.

■ **Congestive heart failure** is the end result of any of these defects.

Heart block

This is an acquired problem. A nerve impulse conduction failure occurs in the specialized heart muscle responsible for maintaining normal rhythm and rate.

Blood clotting defects

■ **Clotting problems** may result from poisoning with Warfarin rat poison. Haemorrhage then occurs, which requires immediate treatment (see first aid section).

■ **Congenital clotting defects** arise if the puppy is born with abnormal blood platelets or clotting factors, both of which are essential in normal clotting.

■ **von Willebrand's disease** is a platelet disorder, found particularly in German Shepherds (see page 103).

Tumours

The spleen, which is a reservoir for blood, is a relatively common site for tumours, especially in older dogs. Splenic tumours can bleed slowly into the abdomen or rupture suddenly, causing collapse. Surgical removal is necessary.

DIGESTIVE SYSTEM DISEASES

Mouth problems

Dental disease

■ **Dental caries** (tooth decay) This is common in people but not so in dogs, unless they eat chocolate or other sweet foods.

■ **Periodontal disease** This inflammation and erosion of the gums around the tooth roots is much more common than dental caries. It is slightly less of a problem in large breeds, such as the German Shepherd, but it certainly does occur.

■ **Dental tartar** This forms on the tooth surfaces and irritates the adjacent gum, causing pain, mouth odour, gum recession and, ultimately, tooth loss. Periodontal disease progression may be prevented in many cases by regular tooth brushing coupled with good diet, large chews and hard biscuits.

■ **Tooth fractures** These can result from trauma in road accidents or if your dog is an enthusiastic stone chewer.

■ **Epulis** This is a benign overgrowth of the gum. Surgical removal is needed.

Salivary cysts

These may occur as swellings under the tongue or neck, resulting from a ruptured salivary duct.

Mouth tumours

These are often highly malignant, growing rapidly and spreading to other organs. First symptoms may be bad breath, increased salivation, and bleeding from the mouth plus difficulties in eating.

■ **Foreign bodies** in the mouth (see first aid, page 129).

Problems causing vomiting

■ **Gastritis**
This is inflammation of the stomach and can result from unsuitable diet, scavenging or infection. The dog repeatedly vomits either

food or yellowish fluid and froth, which may be blood stained.

■ Obstruction of the oesophagus

This leads to regurgitation of food immediately after feeding, and may be caused by small bones or other foreign bodies. Diagnosis is confirmed by X-ray or examination with an endoscope, and treatment must not be delayed.

■ Megoesophagus

This is a defect in the wall of the oesophagus due to faulty nerve control, which leads to ballooning, retention of swallowed food and regurgitation before the food reaches the stomach. It appears to be inherited in some German Shepherd puppies.

■ Obstruction lower down the gut, in the stomach or intestine

This may result from items such as stones,

corks etc. Tumours can also lead to obstructive vomiting. The dog rapidly becomes very ill and the diagnosis is usually confirmed by palpation, X-rays or exploratory surgery.

■ Intussusception

This condition is telescoping of the bowel which can follow diarrhoea, especially in puppies. Surgery is essential.

■ Gastric dilatation (see page 137).

Pancreatic diseases

■ Acute pancreatitis

This is an extremely painful and serious condition requiring intensive therapy. It can be life-threatening.

■ Pancreatic insufficiency

Wasting of the cells of the pancreas which produce digestive enzymes leads to poor

THE DIGESTIVE SYSTEM

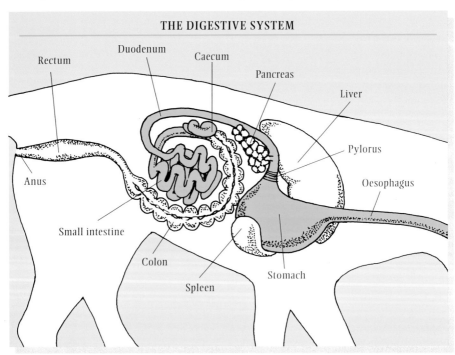

Rectum · Duodenum · Caecum · Pancreas · Liver · Anus · Pylorus · Oesophagus · Small intestine · Colon · Spleen · Stomach

PROBLEMS CAUSING DIARRHOEA

■ **Dietary diarrhoea**

This can occur as a result of sudden changes in diet, scavenging, feeding unsuitable foods or stress (especiallyin pups when they go to their new home).

■ **Pancreatic insufficiency** (see below)

■ **Malabsorption**

This is an uncommon condition which is caused by defective absorption of digested food. Affected dogs have a ravenous appetite, pass bulky, soft faeces, and are underweight. Laboratory tests are often required to confirm the diagnosis.

■ **Enteritis**

This is inflammation of the small intestines which can be caused by infection, e.g. parvovirus, a severe worm burden or food poisoning. Continued diarrhoea leads to dehydration.

■ **Colitis**

An inflammation of the large bowel (colon). The symptoms include straining and frequent defaecation, watery faeces with mucous or blood, and often an otherwise healthy dog.

■ **Tumours of the bowel**

These are more likely to cause vomiting than diarrhoea, but one called lymphosarcoma causes diffuse thickening of the gut lining which may lead to diarrhoea.

digestive function, persistent diarrhoea, weight loss and ravenous appetite. The condition is often diagnosed in dogs of less than two years of age, and is commonly seen in the German Shepherd. Diagnosis is made on clinical symptoms and laboratory testing of blood and faeces.

■ **Diabetes mellitus**

Another function of the pancreas is to manufacture the hormone insulin, which controls blood sugar levels. If insulin is deficient, blood and urine glucose levels rise, both of which can be detected on laboratory testing. Affected animals have an increased appetite and thirst, weight loss and lethargy. If left untreated, the dog may go into a diabetic coma.

■ **Pancreatic tumours**

These are relatively common and are usually highly malignant. Symptoms vary from vomiting, weight loss and signs of abdominal pain to acute jaundice. The prognosis is usually hopeless, and death rapidly occurs.

Liver diseases

■ **Acute hepatitis**

Infectious Canine Hepatitis and Leptospirosis (see infectious diseases). This is not common as most dogs are vaccinated.

■ **Chronic liver failure**

This can be due to heart failure, tumours or cirrhosis. Affected dogs usually lose weight and become depressed, go off their food and may vomit. Diarrhoea and increased thirst are other possible symptoms. The liver may increase or decrease in size, and there is sometimes fluid retention in the abdomen. Jaundice is sometimes apparent. Diagnosis of liver disease depends on symptoms, blood tests, X-rays or ultrasound examination, and possibly liver biopsy.

STRUCTURE OF THE SKIN

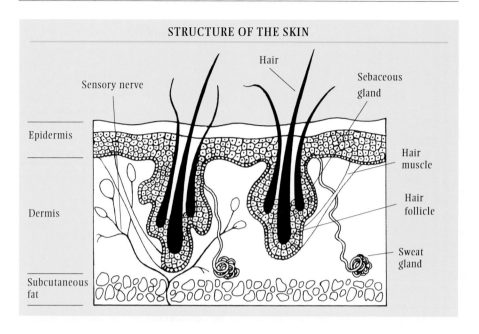

Sensory nerve

Hair

Sebaceous gland

Epidermis

Hair muscle

Hair follicle

Dermis

Sweat gland

Subcutaneous fat

SKIN DISEASES

Itchy skin diseases

Parasites

■ **Fleas** are the most common cause of skin disease, and dogs often become allergic to them. They are dark, fast moving, sideways-flattened insects, about two millimetres long. They spend about two hours a day feeding on the dog, then jump off and spend the rest of the day breeding and laying eggs. They live for about three weeks and can lay fifty eggs a day. Thus each flea may leave behind 1,000 eggs which hatch out in as little as three weeks. It is important to treat the dog and the environment, e.g. his bed, bedding etc. There are many antiparasitic preparations for killing fleas, including sprays, washes, powders and flea collars. Ask your vet for advice on which product to use.

■ **Lice** are less common. They are small, whitish insects crawling very slowly between and up the hairs. They lay eggs on the hair, spend their entire life on the dog and are much easier to treat than fleas. There are effective antiparasitic preparations for killing lice. Again, it is best to consult your vet.

■ **Mange** is caused by a mite (Sarcoptes) which burrows into the skin, causing intense irritation and hair loss. It is very contagious and more common in young dogs. It also spends its entire life on the dog. Your vet may prescribe a antiparasitic wash, or even antibiotics in severe cases.

■ **Bacterial infections**
These are common in the dog and are often secondary to some other skin disease, such as mange or allergies.

■ **Pyoderma** can be an acute, wet, painful area of the skin (wet eczema), or a more persistent infection appearing as ring-like sores. Both are very common in the German Shepherd Dog, especially on the rump. It must not be left untreated.

■ **Furunculosis** is a deeper, more serious infection seen quite often in the German Shepherd Dog.

■ **Contact dermatitis**

This is an itchy reddening of the skin, usually of the abdomen, groin, armpit or feet, where the hair is thinnest and less protective. It can be an allergic response to materials, such as wool, nylon or carpets, or to a direct irritant, such as oil, or a disinfectant.

■ **Lick granuloma**

Ths is a thickened, hairless patch of skin usually on the front of the wrist or the side of the ankle. It is seen quite commonlyin the German Shepherd Dog. It results from constant licking of this area because of boredom or neurosis.

Non-itchy skin diseases

■ **Demodectic mange**

Caused by a congenitally-transmitted parasitic mite, demodectic mange is seen usually in young growing dogs, and causes non-itchy patchy hair loss.

■ **Ticks**

These are parasitic spiders resembling small grey peas, which attach themselves to the skin. They drop off after a week, but should be removed when noticed. Soak them with surgical spirit and pull them out using fine tweezers.

■ **Ringworm**

This is a fungal infection of the hairs and skin causing bald patches. It is transmissible to man. Treatment should be sought as soon as possible.

■ **Hormonal skin disease**

This patchy, symmetrical hair loss is not common in the German Shepherd Dog.

TUMOURS AND CYSTS

■ **Sebaceous cysts**

These are round, painless nodules in the skin and vary from 2 mm ($^1/_8$ in)up to 4 cm (1$^1/_2$in) in diameter. They are common in the German Shepherd Dog.

■ **Warts**

These are quite common in the older dog, and other skin tumours do occur

■ **Anal adenomas**

These frequently develop around the anus in old male dogs. They ulcerate when they are quite small and produce small bleeding points.

DISEASES OF THE FEET

■ **Interdigital eczema**

Dogs readily lick their feet after minor damage, and this makes the feet very wet. Infection then occurs between the pads and may lead to lameness.

■ **Interdigital cysts and abscesses**

These are painful swellings between the toes which may make the dog lame. In most cases the cause is unknown, but sometimes they can be caused by a grass seed penetrating the skin between the toes. The cyst will need to be lanced by the vet and bathed frequently in a warm saline solution.

■ **Foreign body in the pad**

The most common foreign body is a sharp fragment of glass, or a thorn. The dog is usually very lame and the affected pad is painful to the touch. Often an entry point will be seen on the pad. Your vet may be able to remove the foreign body by digital pressure, but in some cases a general anaesthetic may be needed.

STRUCTURE OF THE FOOT

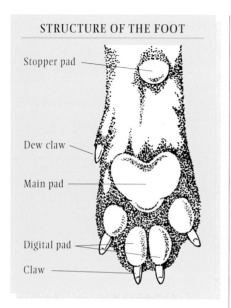

Stopper pad

Dew claw

Main pad

Digital pad

Claw

■ **Nail bed infections**

The toe becomes swollen and painful and the dog becomes lame. If neglected, the bone may become diseased and this can lead to amputation of the affected toe. Always consult your vet as soon as possible so that the infection can be treated with a suitable antibiotic.

DISEASES OF THE ANAL AREA

■ **Anal sac impaction**

This is a very common condition. The anal sacs are scent glands and little used in the dog. If the secretion slowly accumulates in the gland instead of being emptied during defaecation, the over-full anal sac can become itchy. The dog drags his anus along the ground or bites himself around the base of his tail. Unless the sacs are emptied by your vet, an abscess may form.

■ **Anal furunculosis**

(see special health problems, page 103)

EAR DISEASES

Haematoma

A painless, sometimes large, blood blister in the ear flap, usually caused by head shaking due to an ear infection or irritation. It will be replaced by unsightly scar tissue if it is left untreated.

Infection (otitis)

Due to his upright ear flap, and good ventilation of the ear, the German Shepherd Dog is not particularly prone to ear infections. When otitis occurs, a smelly discharge appears, and the dog shakes his head or scratches his ear. If the inner ear is affected, the dog may also show a head tilt or a disturbance in his balance.

■ **Treatment** with antibiotic ear drops is usually successful, but sometimes a surgical operation is needed. The vet must be consulted as there are several possible reasons for ear disease, including ear mites and grass seeds.

EYE DISEASES

Entropion

This is an inherited disease, usually of the young, growing dog. The edge of an eyelid rolls in so that the lashes rub against the surface of the eye, causing irritation of the eyeball. The eye is sore and wet with tears, and often kept closed. Surgical treatment is necessary.

Third eyelid disease

Two problems occur commonly in German Shepherds:

■ **Prolapse of the Harderian gland**

This is a small fleshy mass of tissue behind

the third eyelid. It can become displaced and protrude. Surgical removal is necessary.

■ **Eversion of the third eyelid**
Occasionally in young dogs, especially German Shepherds, the edge of the nictitating membrane rolls outwards due to a kink. It irritates the eye and the kinked tissue should be removed.

■ **Prolapse of the eye**
(see first aid, page 136)

Conjunctivitis

This is a common condition in dogs. The white of the eye appears red and discharges. Possible causes include viruses, bacteria, chemicals, allergies, trauma or foreign bodies.

■ **Treatment** You must consult your vet. He will recommend that the eyes are bathed with warm sterile water, and will prescribe either antibiotics and/or anti-inflammatory drops or ointment.

Keratitis

A very sore inflammation of the cornea, which may appear blue and lose its shiny appearance. It must be bathed and treated with antibiotics and/or anti-inflammatory drugs as directed by your vet.

Corneal ulcer

This is an erosion of part of the surface of the cornea and can follow an injury or keratitis. You should consult your vet. Most ulcers heal with treatment.

Pannus

This is an auto-immune inflammation of the cornea. It occurs most commonly in the German Shepherd Dog and may be inherited. It is treated with anti-inflammatory drops.

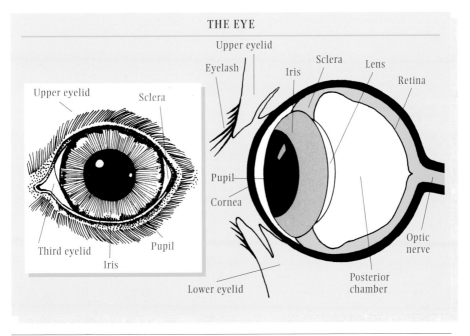

THE EYE

Upper eyelid
Eyelash
Iris
Sclera
Lens
Retina
Upper eyelid
Sclera
Pupil
Cornea
Third eyelid
Pupil
Iris
Optic nerve
Lower eyelid
Posterior chamber

Cataract

An opacity of the lens in one or both eyes. The pupil appears greyish instead of the normal black colour. In advanced cases, the lens looks like a pearl and the dog may be blind. The many causes of cataract include infection, diabetes mellitus, trauma, and inherited causes. Surgical removal is the only treatment.

URINARY SYSTEM DISEASES

Diseases producing increased thirst

■ **Acute kidney failure**
The most common infectious agent producing acute nephritis is Leptospirosis (see infectious diseases, page 105).

■ **Chronic kidney failure**
This is common in old dogs and occurs when persistent damage to the kidney results in toxic substances starting to accumulate in the blood stream. Unfortunately, the prognosis is poor.

Diseases causing blood in the urine

■ **Cystitis**
This is an infection of the bladder. It is more common in bitches because the infection has easy access through the shorter urethra. The clinical signs include increased frequency of urination, straining and sometimes a bloody urine. In all other respects, the dog remains healthy. Treatment is usually with antibiotics.

■ **Urinary calculi or stones**
These can form in either the kidneys or bladder.

■ **Kidney stones** Small kidney stones can enter the ureters causing severe abdominal pain. Surgical removal is necessary.

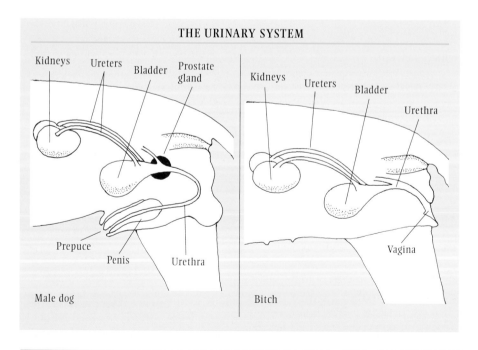

THE URINARY SYSTEM

Kidneys Ureters Bladder Prostate gland

Prepuce Penis Urethra

Male dog

Kidneys Ureters Bladder Urethra

Vagina

Bitch

■ **Bladder stones** Calculi, or bladder stones, are fairly common in both sexes. In the bitch, they are larger and straining is usually the only clinical sign. In the dog, the most common sign is unproductive straining due to urinary obstruction. They can sometimes be dissolved by feeding a special diet, but they may need surgical removal.

■ **Tumours of the bladder**
These tumours can occur but are uncommon. They cause frequent straining and bloody urine, or, by occupying space within the bladder, they cause incontinence.

Incontinence

This occasionally occurs for no apparent reason. Hormones, or medicine to tighten the bladder sphincter, can help.

REPRODUCTIVE ORGAN DISEASES

The male dog

■ **Retained testicle (cryptorchidism)**
Occasionally one or both testicles may fail to descend into the scrotum and remain somewhere along their developmental path. Surgery is advisable to remove retained testicles as they are very likely to develop cancer.

■ **Tumours**
These are fairly common but, fortunately, most are benign. One type of testicular tumour, known as a Sertoli cell tumour, produces female hormones leading to the development of female characteristics.

■ **Prostate disease**
Ths is common in the old dog. Usually a benign enlargement occurs where the prostate slowly increases in size. Hormone treatment or castration helps.

■ **Infection of the penis and sheath (balanitis)**
An increase and discolouration occurs in the discharge from the sheath, and the dog licks his penis more frequently. Consult your vet for advice on how to treat it.

■ **Paraphimosis**
Prolapse of the penis (see page 120)

■ **Castration**
This is of value in the treatment of many behavioural problems. Excessive sexual activity, such as mounting cushions or other dogs, and territorial urination may be eliminated by castration, as may certain types of aggression and the desire to escape and wander.

The bitch

■ **Pyometra**
This is a common and serious disease of the older bitch, although bitches that have had puppies seem less likely to develop it. The treatment of choice for this is usually an ovariohysterectomy.

■ **Mastitis**
An infection of the mammary glands, mastitis occurs usually in lactating bitches. The affected glands become swollen, hard, and painful (see page 124).

MAMMARY TUMOURS

These are common in the older entire bitch. Most are benign, but, where malignant, they can grow rapidly and spread to other organs. Early surgical removal of any lump is advisable because of the danger of malignancy.

- **False or pseudo pregnancy** (see page 120)
- **Birth control**
- **Hormone therapy** Several preparations, injections and tablets, are available to prevent or postpone the bitch's heat period.
- **Spaying (ovariohysterectomy)** This is an operation to remove the uterus and ovaries, usually performed when the bitch is not on heat.

NERVOUS SYSTEM DISEASES

The nervous system consists of two parts:

1 **The central nervous system (CNS)** – the brain and the spinal cord which runs through the vertebral column.

2 **The peripheral nervous system** – all the nerves that connect the CNS to the organs of the body.

Diseases of the nervous system are outlined below.

- **Canine distemper virus** (see page 105)
- **Vestibular syndrome**
This is a fairly common condition of the older dog, and affects that part of the brain that controls balance. There is a sudden head tilt to the affected side, often flicking movements of the eyes called nystagmus, and the dog may fall or circle to that side. Many dogs will recover slowly but the condition may recur.
- **Slugbait (Metaldehyde) poisoning**
The dog appears 'drunk', uncoordinated, and may have convulsions. There is no specific treatment, but sedation will often lead to recovery in a large dog like the German Shepherd Dog.
- **Epilepsy**
This is a nervous disorder that is seen more commonly in the German Shepherd than in other breeds. It is covered fully in Chapter Six (see page 103).

BONE, MUSCLE AND JOINT DISEASES

Note: X-rays are usually necessary to confirm any diagnosis involving bone.

- **Bone infection (osteomyelitis)**
This usually occurs after an injury, such as a bite, or where a broken bone protrudes through the skin. Signs are pain, heat and swelling over the site, and if a limb bone is affected, there can be severe lameness.
- **Fractures**
Any break or crack in a bone is called a fracture. When a vet repairs a fracture, his aim is to replace the fractured ends of bone into their normal position and then to immobilize the bone for four to six weeks. Depending on the bone, and type of fracture, there are several methods available:
- Cage rest
- External casts
- Surgery to perform internal fixation, e.g. by plating or pinning
- **Bone tumours**
These are not common, except in the giant breeds, but they are known to occur in the German Shepherd. The most common sites are the radius, humerus and femur. Bone tumours are very painful, and they tend to be malignant and spread to other parts of the body early in the course of the disease. Amputation of the limb will remove the primary tumour but, as it may have already spread to other areas, it is often not feasible. Radiotherapy and chemotherapy are not normally successful.
- **Sprains**
A sprain is an inflammation of an over-stretched joint. The joint is hot, swollen, and painful, and the dog is lame. Sprains are usually treated with rest, cold compresses and

THE SKELETON

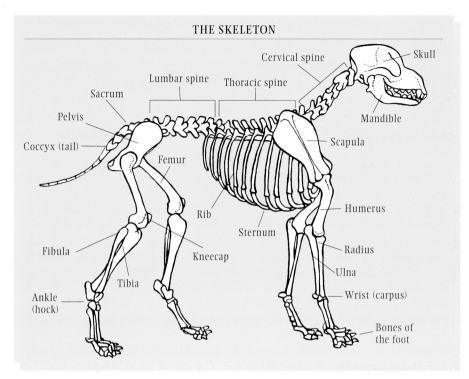

Cervical spine

Skull

Lumbar spine

Thoracic spine

Sacrum

Pelvis

Mandible

Coccyx (tail)

Scapula

Femur

Humerus

Rib

Sternum

Fibula

Radius

Kneecap

Ulna

Tibia

Ankle (hock)

Wrist (carpus)

Bones of the foot

maybe a mild, pain-killing drug. More severe strains may require supporting bandages and anti-inflammatory drugs.

■ **Cruciate ligament rupture**

When these rupture, as a result of a severe sprain, the stifle or knee joint is destabilized and the dog becomes instantly and severely lame on that leg. This usually occurs in middle-aged, overweight dogs. Surgical repair is usually necessary.

■ **Arthritis or degenerative joint disease**

Unfortunately, this is common in the German Shepherd Dog, where it invariably follows hip dysplasia, or an ununited anconeus process in the elbow. It results in thickening of the joint capsule, the formation of abnormal new bone around the edges of the joint and, sometimes, wearing of the joint cartilage. The joint

becomes enlarged and painful, and has a reduced range of movement. It tends to occur in the older dog and is usually a problem of the hips, stifles and elbows. There is no cure, and treatment is usually with anti-inflammatory drugs with the aim of providing pain relief.

■ **Spondylitis**

This is arthritis of the spine. It is quite common in the older German Shepherd Dog and causes weakness and stiffness of the hindquarters. Again, treatment is with anti-inflammatory drugs, but there is no cure.

■ **Osteochondritis dissicans (OCD)**

This is a degeneration of the cartilage in certain joints of young dogs under a year old, which is seen in the larger breeds such as the German Shepherd. Surgical removal of the affected cartilage is usually necessary.

Hip dysplasia (HD)

Hip dysplasia is the commonest and most serious of the developmental abnormalities of the German Shepherd Dog. In a normal dog, the hip is a 'ball and socket' joint and allows a wide range of movement. The rounded end at the top of the femur, the femoral head, fits tightly into the acetabulum in the pelvis, a deep, cup-shaped socket. Hip dysplasia is the development of a shallow acetabulum, an irregular, distorted head of the femur, and slackness of the joint ligaments. Excessive movement can and does occur between the femur and the pelvis, and this leads to a malfunctioning painful joint, which will gradually become arthritic.

It is known to be inherited but there are other factors involved, such as poor nutrition, too much exercise, or even being overweight during the rapid growth phase of the young dog.

- **Symptoms in puppies**

A puppy developing severe hip dysplasia may have great difficulty walking, and particularly standing up from a sitting position, which he may find painful and cry out. He may appear to sway when running or, characteristically, use both hind legs together in a bunny hop. These signs may be present as young as five months old. Mildly affected puppies may show no signs at all at this stage, but at about eight years of age begin to develop arthritis.

- **Diagnosis**

Your vet will suspect hip dysplasia in a German Shepherd Dog with the above symptoms at the right age. Confirmation is by manipulation of the suspect joint and X-ray.

- **Hip dysplasia scheme**

All German Shepherd Dogs, of both sexes, intended for breeding should be X-rayed at not less than one year of age. In the UK, the British Veterinary Association and the Kennel Club have for many years run a joint scheme (the BVA/KC

hip dysplasia scheme) based on hip scoring, and the vet submits the X-ray, bearing the KC registration number of the dog, to the scheme. Each hip is scored from 0 to 54, making a total of 108 maximum between the two hips. The lower the score the better, 0:0 is the best possible.

The average combined score for all the German Shepherd Dog X-rays submitted so far (over 21,000) is 18.6, and no-one should breed from a dog with a higher hip score than this if HD is ever to be reduced or eliminated from the breed. Anyone buying a puppy should ensure that both parents have been X-rayed and achieved a low score. This is not, of course, an absolute guarantee that the puppy will not develop hip dysplasia, but it should considerably reduce the chances.

- **Treatment**

If the hip dysplasia is diagnosed at an early stage, and is mild, a combination of anabolic steroids, restricted exercise, and a slightly underweight dog during the growth phase will often lead to a sound adult dog. He may, however, only be able to indulge in a limited amount of exercise during his life. Too much at this stage may lead to arthritis later. In more severe cases, one of several available surgical techniques will be needed, but the dog will never be as agile as an unaffected dog.

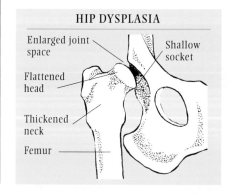

HIP DYSPLASIA

Enlarged joint space

Shallow socket

Flattened head

Thickened neck

Femur

8

BREEDING

If properly planned, breeding a litter from your own dog or bitch can be rewarding and great fun. The secret of successful breeding is to use good stock, to plan ahead so you have plenty of time, to understand that you could be unsuccessful, and to be aware in advance of the needs of the bitch and puppies. German Shepherds can have large litters – ten puppies is not unusual – so you do need to make sure you can find good homes for this number.

Action prior to mating

1 Locate the right dog of the opposite sex. He will be of good and known temperament, and be free of inherited or contagious disease.

■ As a breeder of German Shepherds, hip dysplasia, an inherited defect of the hip joint, is the main problem that you could pass on to the puppies. Therefore your own bitch or dog, and the prospective mate, should have their

hips X-rayed before breeding (see page 102). Although low-scoring parents are not an absolute guarantee that the puppies will not suffer from hip dysplasia, they will considerably reduce the chances.

■ The temperament of both parents is all important. Remember that the puppies will almost certainly be going to caring family homes, and with a big breed like the German Shepherd, it is essential that they end up well balanced, calm, sociable individuals.

2 Check both pedigrees (family trees) to ensure that you are not breeding from a dog and bitch who are related too closely.

3 If possible, allow the dogs to get to know each other before mating.

MATING

A German Shepherd bitch should not be mated until she matures, usually at one and a half to two years old. The male would normally be at

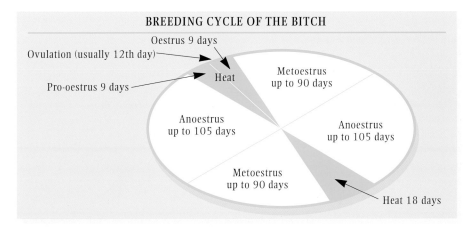

BREEDING CYCLE OF THE BITCH

Oestrus 9 days
Ovulation (usually 12th day)
Pro-oestrus 9 days
Heat
Metoestrus up to 90 days
Anoestrus up to 105 days
Anoestrus up to 105 days
Metoestrus up to 90 days
Heat 18 days

FALSE OR PSEUDO PREGNANCY

This occurs in most bitches about eight to twelve weeks after oestrus at the stage when the bitch would be lactating had she been pregnant. The signs vary and include:
- Poor appetite
- Lethargy
- Milk production
- Nest building
- Aggressiveness
- Attachment to a substitute puppy, which is often a squeaky toy

Once a bitch has had a false pregnancy, she is likely to have one after each heat period.
- **Treatment,** if needed, is by hormones, and prevention is by a hormone injection, or tablets, or an ovariohysterectomy.

least that age. The bitch comes into heat, on average, twice a year, for about three weeks at a time. The vulva swells, and bleeding starts; initially fairly runny, this becomes darker and more tacky as she approaches ovulation. This fertile time is usually ten to twelve days after the heat starts.

When she is ready to accept the male, she will stand with her tail raised to one side. The male mounts the bitch and the penis is usually locked into position inside the female, producing the so-called 'tie'. After a minute or so, the male lifts one hind leg over her back and places it on the ground. The two dogs stand back to back for up to twenty minutes, until the penis subsides and they can separate. This tie ensures that the maximum amount of sperm

reaches the uterus and increases the chances of fertilization. A tie is not essential and pregnancies frequently result from 'slip' services where ejaculation occurs without a tie.
- With a novice bitch, it may be necessary to hold her gently while she is mated to reassure her.
- It is advisable to mate the two dogs at least twice on successive days, but a greater success rate is achieved if the dogs are allowed to run together on several successive days.

Mismating

If an unwanted mating has occurred, your vet can give the bitch a hormone injection to prevent fertilization. This must be given within three days of the mating.

Bitch will not mate

- The stage of heat may not be correct. If in doubt, your vet can take blood samples or vaginal swabs to ascertain whether she is at the correct stage to mate.
- Failure to complete the mating may be due to a stricture within the vagina. Or the bitch may have unrelated problems, such as hip pain. If she shows signs of discomfort and moves away, consult your vet.

No pregnancy

- Try again at the next heat and consider a different male. There may be nothing wrong individually with either the dog or bitch but together they may be incompatible.

Paraphimosis

This is a prolonged erection of the penis which is unable to retract back into the sheath after mating. It becomes very swollen due to constriction by the sheath. The exposed penis should be bathed in cool sterile water to reduce it in size, and lubrication with petroleum jelly or soap should make it possible to pull the sheath forward over the penis. If correction proves impossible, veterinary help is needed.

PREGNANCY

Pregnancy is normally sixty-three days. For the first three weeks, there is little change in the bitch. She may be quieter than normal and look plump. The teats and breasts may begin to enlarge.

Diet during pregnancy

Food intake should be increased and the bitch should be put on a balanced, calcium-rich diet. There are excellent commercial complete diets available for this purpose. Ideally, a 'growth formula' diet should be introduced at the sixth week of pregnancy, and should be continued throughout pregnancy and lactation, so that the bitch and her puppies are on the same diet from late pregnancy onwards. About a week before she is due to give birth (whelp), milk may start to ooze from the teats.

Preparation for whelping

■ **A whelping box** should be prepared in advance. There will be a lot of discharge during the birth and it is a good idea to line the box with several layers of newspaper which can be removed gradually as they become soiled.

■ The bitch should be able to stretch out in either direction, with the safety bar in place.

SIGNS OF PREGNANCY

■ About four weeks after mating, your vet may be able to detect pregnancy by feeling the bitch's abdomen.

■ There is also a blood test that can detect pregnancy at this stage.

■ Ultrasound examination is now available in an increasing number of veterinary practices, and can be used to detect pregnancy after twenty-eight days.

■ At about six weeks, the bitch's abdomen begins to increase in size, and the teats and mammary glands begin to enlarge. She may become quieter but her appetite remains good.

■ **An infra-red heat source** directly over the whelping area is essential to prevent hypothermia developing in the puppies, because they are unable to regulate their own body temperature until they are about ten to fourteen days old.

■ **The whelping room** should be warm and quiet, and supervision of the whelping should be by someone the bitch knows and trusts.

WHELPING

1 Labour starts gradually, the bitch just appearing restless. She usually bed-makes by tearing up newspaper or scattering blankets around. This initial stage can last for up to twenty four hours but it is usually much shorter. Her temperature will drop from 38.5°C (101.5°F) to about 36°C (97°F). Towards the end of this period, the contractions begin.

2 These contractions gradually increase in frequency until the bitch is contracting several times each minute, and a water bag appears at the vulva. A puppy is usually born within twenty minutes of the onset of regular rhythmical contractions, but this can take up to two hours in a normal whelping. From this stage onwards, the interval between puppies varies enormously, even up to twelve hours. However, an interval of ten to sixty minutes between each puppy is more likely.

3 The bitch will usually lick the puppy immediately on birth. This ruptures the bag and revives the puppy who will begin to cry as he fills his lungs for the first time. If the bitch ignores the puppy or seems confused, you must gently tear the membranes from around him, hold him in a towel, wipe out the mouth and vigorously rub the puppy to stimulate breathing.

4 If the placenta is still attached to the puppy, the umbilical cord should be tied with cotton about 4 cm (1 1/2 in) from the puppy and then carefully cut with scissors on the side of the knot away from the puppy. Gently place the puppy on a teat to begin suckling. Do not pull on the umbilical cord as this can lead to an umbilical hernia in the puppy.

5 If the placenta (afterbirth) is passed, it will usually be eaten by the bitch. This should be encouraged. However, it may become detached and remain inside the uterus, slowly disintegrating and being expelled from the uterus as a darkish discharge over the next few weeks. This is perfectly normal.

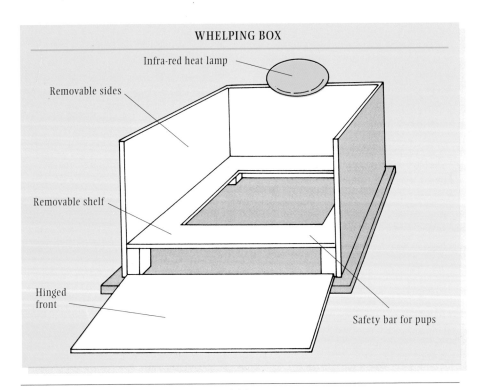

WHELPING BOX

Infra-red heat lamp

Removable sides

Removable shelf

Hinged front

Safety bar for pups

COMPLICATIONS

Primary inertia
This is when the bitch fails to start
contracting. If whelping does not follow
within twenty four hours of the onset of
signs of restlessness, if the bitch is more
than one day overdue, or if a green vaginal
discharge is noticed, the bitch should be
examined by a vet.

Secondary inertia
This usually follows a prolonged unproductive
labour where due to an obstruction, called a
dystocia, birth cannot take place and the bitch
becomes exhausted. This can be caused by an
abnormally positioned or sized foetus (foetal
dystocia), or by a uterine obstruction
(maternal dystocia). An obstructing puppy
may be removed manually by the vet, or a
Caesarean section may be necessary.

Dystocia
A dystocia is suspected where the bitch has
been contracting unproductively for over two
hours. In this case the vet must always be
called. Possible causes include:

■ A previous pelvic fracture causing a
narrowing of the birth canal
■ A twisted uterus
■ An over-large puppy
■ A congenitally abnormal puppy
■ A malpresentation.

Puppies are normally born either head and
forelegs first (anterior presentation) or tail
and back legs first (posterior presentation).
Note: Any variation on this is called a
malpresentation and can cause foetal
dystocia. Two common examples are:

■ **Breech presentation** The tail is coming
first but the hindlegs are tucked up forwards
under the puppy's abdomen. This enlarges
the buttocks of the puppy and causes an
obstruction.

■ **Head first with forelegs pointing
backwards** Delivery is prevented because
the shoulder area is enlarged.
Note: all these obstructions will require
veterinary attention, assisted birth or, if
necessary, a Caesarean section.

6 The bitch will pay some attention to each
puppy when he is born, but she will not be
very interested in the litter until whelping is
complete, when a change in attitude is obvious.
She will brighten up, clean herself thoroughly
and begin to look after the puppies in earnest.

POSTNATAL: THE BITCH

Feeding

During the lactation phase, the pups make
maximum demands on the bitch, and it is

essential that she is fed a fully nutritious diet.
Simply supplementing with calcium is not
enough. The best diet is a quality complete-
growth diet formulated specially for the lactating
bitch, and she should be fed almost to demand.

Possible problems

■ **Vaginal discharge** A greenish brown
discharge is normal for the first few days and
may continue for several weeks.
■ **Post whelping metritis** This is very
serious. The bitch is very ill with a raised

EXERCISE

During the first few days she will not want to be away from the pups for long and will certainly not require exercise to any degree. She will, of course, require frequent access to the garden or outside for toileting purposes, and may appreciate a short walk for a change of scene. She may or may not want your company!

temperature, and has a profuse, foul vaginal discharge. A vet should be consulted without delay.

■ **No milk** The puppies fail to thrive and cry continuously. It is essential to supplement feeding with a foster feeding bottle and synthetic milk available from your vet.

■ **Mastitis** This can occur in over-engorged mammary glands.Check daily that no breasts are sore, very hard or hot.

■ **Behavioural change** The bitch may become very protective of her puppies and be aggressive to her owners. She should be left alone to start with, but the pups must be checked regularly in her absence. After a few days, her worries usually subside and she becomes trusting again. If handling is necessary, for instance to supplement the pups, a muzzle may be necessary.

■ **Aggression to puppies** This can occur initially, and the bitch must be muzzled or the pups separated. Usually this is caused by fright or confusion, or is due to displaced excessive cleaning. Hold the puppies on to her forcibly to be suckled for a while, and she will normally accept them.

■ **Eclampsia** This is a very serious condition and can be fatal. The blood calcium

level of the bitch becomes too low due to the demands of the pups on her milk and she begins to show nervous symptoms. Initially she starts to twitch or shiver and appears unsteady. This rapidly progresses to staggering, then convulsions. The vet must be contacted immediately as an injection of calcium is essential to save the life of the bitch.

The pups should be partially or completely weaned to ensure the eclampsia does not recur. The time of onset varies but it is usually seen when the pups are about three weeks old and are making maximum demands on her.

With large litters, supplementing the puppies' feeding to relieve the load on the dam would seem to be a logical approach to prevention, although other factors can be involved.

■ **Squashed puppy** This accident can be prevented by using the correct whelping box design.

Hypothermia

This is the commonest cause of death in unweaned puppies. The whelping area or box must be kept warm by a direct heat source, such as an infra-red lamp or an electric blanket. A warm room is not usually sufficient.

CARING FOR THE PUPPIES

Days one and two

■ Check for obvious congenital abnormalities such as hare lip, cleft palate and undershot or overshot jaws. If in doubt, the vet should be asked to attend.

■ Ensure that the puppies all suckle the bitch on the first day. This is important as her first milk (colostrum) is rich in antibodies and enables them to withstand infections during their first six to twelve weeks of life.

■ Make sure that the puppies are having enough to drink. A quiet litter is usually a happy, well-fed litter. If any puppies are weaker, it may be necessary to supplement them with synthetic bitch's milk using a foster feeder bottle.

Days three to five

■ If dew claws are present on the hind legs, German Shepherd Dogs should have them removed at three to five days old. They often snag and bleed in adult life. Front dew claws are usually left on.

Days five to fourteen

■ **Fading Puppy Syndrome** Puppies can fade and die for no apparent reason. If this happens, it is essential that the vet is consulted. A dead puppy is useful for a post mortem examination. The cause may be hypothermia, infection, lack of food, lack of colostrum, trauma from the bitch, roundworms or any stress.

■ The eyes open at ten to fourteen days, and abnormalities can be noticed now. For example, an eye may be absent, or smaller than normal. These are both congenital abnormalities, but are not common in the German Shepherd.

■ Treat the puppies for roundworms at fourteen days – consult your vet.

Days fourteen to twenty one

■ The pups become more mobile and at three weeks they are quite lively and capable of wandering out of the whelping area. This is a

WORMING

Roundworm larvae are passed to the puppies while they are still in the uterus via the placenta, and after birth through the milk. This can be minimized by giving a larvicidal wormer to the bitch during pregnancy and lactation. Your vet should be consulted for details of dose and timing. In addition, the bitch should be dosed each time the puppies are wormed to prevent the build-up of a roundworm burden within the litter and its environment.

useful time to begin socializing them by frequent handling and exposure to household events and noises. The bed should be moved from time to time to create an environmental challenge for the puppies.

Days twenty-one to forty-two

■ At twenty-one days, weaning can begin. The pups should be taught to lap proprietary or skimmed cow's milk to start with. Soon they can be tried with porridge-style cereals, scraped fish or finely minced chicken. Feed them several times a day, but at this stage they will also be suckling the bitch.

■ By twenty-eight days, they should have progressed on to four or five small meals a day, preferably of a good quality, commercial complete puppy-growth formula food. Alternatively, meat (fresh or canned puppy food) with, say, soaked human or puppy cereals can be given. A balanced vitamin and mineral supplement should be added only to home-prepared food as growth-formula food contains the right balance already.

■ At twenty eight days, the puppies should be wormed again and thereafter at intervals of two weeks up to the age of three months, using a safe effective veterinary wormer. Thereafter worming should be carried out monthly up to six months of age, and then two to four times a year for the rest of their lives.

■ The puppies should be handled gently, but often, by all family members, and exposed to as many household noises as possible. Their environment should be quite challenging and rich in toys, cardboard boxes, balls and other playthings.

LEAVING HOME

The best age for a German Shepherd puppy to adapt to a new family is between six and eight weeks of age, so this is the age at which you should aim to sell the pups. Remember that a puppy will make a better pet if you and your family have been gently playing with him and handling him. Before parting with a puppy you should:

■ Interview the prospective purchasers to ensure that they will give him a caring home and that a German Shepherd Dog will suit their lifestyle.

■ Ensure that the puppy is fit and well.

■ Prepare a diet sheet to give to the new owners.

■ Ask your vet whether the puppies should have their first vaccination. If this is done, hand over the vaccination certificate and tell the new owners when the next one is due.

■ Inform the new owners when the puppy was wormed, with what, and when the next dose is due.

■ Prepare the pedigree form, and hand it over.

■ Take out a temporary pet health insurance policy on the puppy. This lasts for six weeks and the new owner should be advised to continue it. It relieves you of the worry of any unforeseen illness or problem in the first few weeks after purchase. It is not expensive and your vet will give you details. In Great Britain, registration of puppies with the Kennel Club now carries free pet insurance for the first six weeks. Other schemes exist whereby your vet can issue the new owner with a free month's instant pet insurance cover at the time of vaccination.

■ Above all, emphasise the need for early socialization with people, dogs, cats and other animals, such as sheep, and early exposure to normal household noises, such as washing machines and vacuum cleaners, and traffic noise.

CHAPTER NINE

FIRST AID, ACCIDENTS AND EMERGENCIES

First aid is the emergency care given to a dog suffering injury or illness of sudden onset.

AIMS OF FIRST AID

1 Keep the dog alive.
2 Prevent unnecessary suffering.
3 Prevent further injury.

RULES OF FIRST AID

1

Keep calm. If you panic you will be unable to help effectively.

2

Contact a vet as soon as possible. Advice given over the telephone may be life-saving.

3

Avoid injury to yourself. A distressed or injured animal may bite so use a muzzle if necessary (see muzzling, page 138).

4

Control haemorrhage. Excessive blood loss can lead to severe shock and death (see haemorrhage, page 131),

5

Maintain an airway. Failure to breathe or obtain adequate oxygen can lead to brain damage or loss of life within five minutes (see airway obstruction and artificial respiration, page 129).

COMMON ACCIDENTS AND EMERGENCIES

The following common accidents and emergencies all require first aid action. In an emergency, your priorities are to keep the dog alive and comfortable until he can be examined by a vet. In many cases, there is effective action that you can take immediately to help preserve your dog's health and life.

SHOCK AND ROAD ACCIDENTS

SHOCK

This is a serious clinical syndrome which can cause death. Shock can follow road accidents, severe burns, electrocution, extremes of heat and cold, heart failure, poisoning, severe fluid loss, reactions to drugs, insect stings or snake bite.

SIGNS OF SHOCK
- Weakness or collapse
- Pale gums
- Cold extremities, e.g. feet and ears
- Weak pulse and rapid heart
- Rapid, shallow breathing

RECOMMENDED ACTION

1
Act immediately. Give cardiac massage (see page 130) and/or artificial respiration (see page 129) if necessary, after checking for a clear airway.

2
Keep the dog flat and warm. Control external haemorrhage (page 131).

3
Veterinary treatment is essential thereafter.

ROAD ACCIDENTS

Injuries resulting from a fast-moving vehicle colliding with an animal can be very serious. Road accidents may result in:
- Death
- Head injuries
- Spinal damage
- Internal haemorrhage, bruising and rupture of major organs, e.g. liver, spleen, kidneys
- Fractured ribs and lung damage, possibly resulting in haemothorax (blood in the chest cavity) or pneumothorax (air in the chest cavity)
- Fractured limbs with or without nerve damage
- External haemorrhage, wounds, tears and bruising

RECOMMENDED ACTION

1
Assess the situation and move the dog to a safe position. Use a blanket to transport him and keep him flat.

2
Check for signs of life: feel for a heart beat (see cardiac massage, page 130), and watch for the rise and fall of the chest wall.

3
If the dog is breathing, treat as for shock (see above). If he is not breathing but there is a heart beat, give artificial respiration, after checking for airway obstruction. Consider the use of a muzzle (see muzzling, page 138).

4
Control external haemorrhage (see haemorrhage, page 131).

5
Keep the dog warm and flat at all times, and seek veterinary help.

AIRWAY OBSTRUCTION

■ **FOREIGN BODY IN THE THROAT,** e.g. a ball.

■ **FOLLOWING A ROAD ACCIDENT,** or convulsion, blood, saliva or vomit in the throat may obstruct breathing.

RECOMMENDED ACTION

1

This is an acute emergency. Do not try to pull out the object. Push it upwards and forwards from behind the throat so that it moves from its position, where it is obstructing the larynx, into the mouth.

2

The dog should now be able to breathe. Remove the object from his mouth.

RECOMMENDED ACTION

1

Pull the tongue forwards and clear any obstruction with your fingers.

2

Then, with the dog on his side, extend the head and neck forwards to maintain a clear airway.

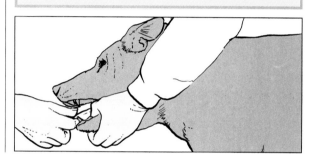

DROWNING

RECOMMENDED ACTION

1

Out of the water, remove collar and place dog on his side with his head lower than his body.

2

With hands, apply firm downward pressure on chest at five-second intervals.

ARTIFICIAL RESPIRATION

The method for helping a dog which has a clear airway but cannot breathe.

RECOMMENDED ACTION

Use mouth-to-mouth resuscitation by cupping your hands over his nose and mouth and blowing into his nostrils every five seconds.

CARDIAC MASSAGE

This is required if your dog's heart fails.

RECOMMENDED ACTION

1

With the dog lying on his right side, feel for a heart beat with your fingers on the chest wall behind the dog's elbows on his left side.

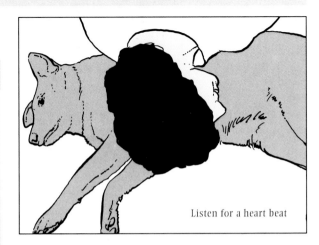

Listen for a heart beat

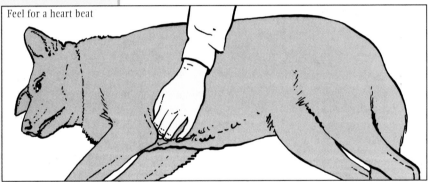

Feel for a heart beat

2

If you feel nothing, squeeze rhythmically with your palms, placing one hand on top of the other, as shown, at two-second intervals, pressing down hard.

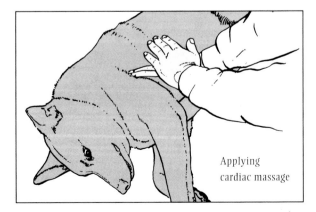

Applying cardiac massage

HAEMORRHAGE

Severe haemorrhage must be controlled, as it leads to a precipitous fall in blood pressure and the onset of shock. Haemorrhage is likely to result from deep surface wounds, or internal injuries, e.g. following a road accident.

■ FOR SURFACE WOUNDS

RECOMMENDED ACTION

Locate the bleeding point and apply pressure either with:
■ **Your thumb** or
■ **A pressure bandage** (preferred method) or
■ **A tourniquet**

1 **Pressure bandage** Use a pad of gauze, cotton wool or cloth against the wound and tightly bandage around it. In the

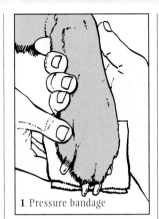

1 Pressure bandage

absence of a proper dressing, use a clean handkerchief or scarf.

2 If the bleeding continues, apply another dressing on top of the first.

1 **Tourniquet** (on limbs and tail) Tie a narrow piece of cloth, a neck tie or dog lead tightly

Tourniquet

around the limb, nearer to the body than the wound itself.

2 Using a pencil or stick within the knot, twist until it becomes tight enough to stop the blood flow.

3 **Important**: you must seek veterinary assistance as soon as possible.

Note: Tourniquets should be applied for no longer than fifteen minutes at a time, or tissue death may result.

■ FOR INTERNAL BLEEDING

RECOMMENDED ACTION

1 You should keep the animal quiet and warm, and minimize any movement.

2 **Important**: you must seek veterinary assistance as soon as possible.

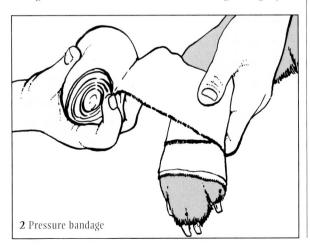

2 Pressure bandage

SHOCK AND ROAD ACCIDENTS

WOUNDS

These may result from road accidents, dog fights, sharp stones or glass, etc. Deep wounds may cause serious bleeding, bone or nerve damage.

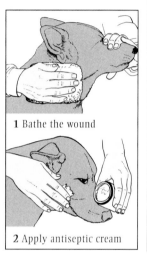

1 Bathe the wound

2 Apply antiseptic cream

RECOMMENDED ACTION

1
Deal with external bleeding (see haemorrhage, page 131) and keep the dog quiet before seeking veterinary attention.

2
Cut feet or pads should be bandaged to prevent further blood loss.

3
Minor cuts, abrasions and bruising should be bathed with warm salt solution (one

5ml teaspoonful per 550ml (1 pint) of water). They should be protected from further injury or contamination. Apply some antiseptic cream, if necessary.

4
If in doubt, ask your vet to check in case the wound needs suturing or antibiotic therapy, particularly if caused by fighting. Even minor cuts and punctures can be complicated by the presence of a foreign body.

FRACTURES

Broken bones, especially in the legs, often result from road accidents. Be careful when lifting and transporting the affected dog.

■ **LEG FRACTURES**

RECOMMENDED ACTION

1 Broken lower leg bones can sometimes be straightened gently, bandaged and then taped or tied with string to a make-shift splint, e.g. a piece of wood or rolled-up newspaper or cardboard.

2 Otherwise, support the leg to prevent any movement. Take the dog to the vet immediately.

■ **OTHER FRACTURES**
These may be more difficult to diagnose. If you suspect a fracture, transport your dog very gently with great care, and get him to the vet.

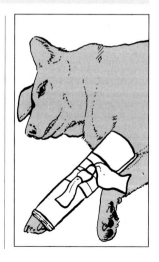

OTHER ACCIDENTS AND EMERGENCIES

COLLAPSE

This may be accompanied by loss of consciousness, but not in every case.

POSSIBLE CAUSES

- Head trauma, e.g. following a road accident
- Heart failure
- Stroke
- Hyperthermia (heat stroke)
- Hypothermia (cold)
- Hypocalcaemia (low calcium)
- Shock

- Spinal fractures
- Asphyxia (interference with breathing)
- Electrocution
- Poisoning

Note: you should refer to the relevant section for further details of these problems.

RECOMMENDED ACTION

1 The collapsed animal must be moved with care to avoid further damage.

2 Gently slide him on his side onto a blanket or coat.

3 Check he is breathing, and then keep him quiet and warm until you obtain professional help.

4 If he is not breathing, administer artificial respiration immediately, after checking for a clear airway (see page 129)

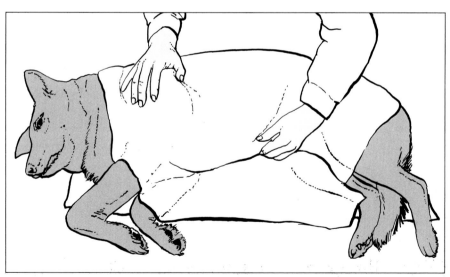

OTHER ACCIDENTS AND EMERGENCIES

CONVULSIONS (FITS OR SEIZURES)

These are very alarming to dog owners. Uncontrolled spasms, 'paddling' of legs, loss of consciousness, sometimes salivation and involuntary urination or defaecation occur. Most convulsions only last a few minutes, but the dog is often confused and dazed afterwards.

POSSIBLE CAUSE

- Poisoning
- Head injuries
- Brain tumours
- Liver and kidney disease
- Meningitis
- Epilepsy
- Low blood glucose, e.g. in diabetes, or low blood calcium, e.g. in eclampsia

RECOMMENDED ACTION

1 Unless he is in a dangerous situation, do not attempt to hold the dog, but protect him from damaging himself.

2 Do not give him anything by mouth.

3 Try to keep him quiet, cool and in a darkened room until he sees the vet.

4 If you have to move him, cover him with a blanket first.

HEART FAILURE

This is not as common in dogs as in humans. Affected dogs faint, usually during exercise, and lose consciousness. The mucous membranes appear pale or slightly blue.

RECOMMENDED ACTION

1 Cover the dog in a blanket, lie him on his side.

2 Massage his chest behind the elbows (see cardiac massage, page 130).

3 When he recovers, take him straight to the vet.

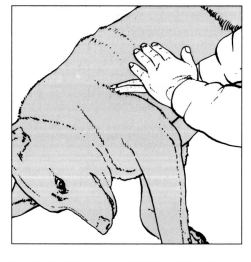

1 An affected dog should be covered with a blanket and laid on his side.
2 Apply cardiac massage, pressing down firmly at two-second intervals.

HEAT-STROKE

This occurs in hot weather, especially when dogs have been left in cars with insufficient ventilation. Affected animals are extremely distressed, panting and possibly collapsed. They can die rapidly. A heat-stroke case should be treated as an acute emergency.

RECOMMENDED ACTION

1 Place the dog in a cold bath or run cold water over his body until his temperature is in the normal range.

2 Offer water with added salt (one 5ml teaspoonful per half litre/18 fl oz water).

3 Treatment for shock may be necessary (see page 128).

ELECTROCUTION

This is most likely to occur in a bored puppy who chews through a cable. Electrocution may kill him outright or lead to delayed shock.

■ **DO NOT TOUCH HIM BEFORE YOU SWITCH OFF THE ELECTRICITY SOURCE.**

RECOMMENDED ACTION

1 If he is not breathing, begin artificial respiration immediately (see page 129) and keep him warm.

2 Contact your vet; if he survives he will need treatment for shock (see page 128).

BURNS AND SCALDS

POSSIBLE CAUSES
■ Spilled hot drinks, boiling water or fat.
■ Friction, chemical and electrical burns.

RECOMMENDED ACTION

1 Immediately apply running cold water and, thereafter, cold compresses, ice packs or packets of frozen peas to the affected area.

2 Veterinary attention is essential in most cases.

SNAKE BITE

This is due to the adder in Great Britain. Signs are pain accompanied by a soft swelling around two puncture wounds, usually on either the head, neck or limbs. Trembling, collapse, shock and even death can ensue.

RECOMMENDED ACTION

1 Do not let the dog walk; carry him to the car.

2 Keep him warm, and take him immediately to the vet.

FOREIGN BODIES

■ **IN THE MOUTH**
Sticks or bones wedged between the teeth cause frantic pawing at the mouth and salivation.

RECOMMENDED ACTION

Remove the foreign body with your fingers or pliers, using a wooden block placed between the dog's canine teeth if possible to aid the safety of this procedure. Some objects have to be removed under general anaesthesia.
Note: a ball in the throat is dealt with in airway obstruction (see page 129), and is a critical emergency.

■ **FISH HOOKS**
Never try to pull these out, wherever they are.

RECOMMENDED ACTION

Cut the end with pliers and then push the barbed end through the skin and out.

■ **IN THE FOOT**
Glass, thorns or splinters can penetrate the pads or soft skin, causing pain, and infection if neglected.

RECOMMENDED ACTION

Soak the foot in warm salt.

water and then use a sharp sterilized needle or pair of tweezers to extract the foreign body. If this is not possible, take your dog to the vet who will remove it under local or general anaesthetic if necessary.

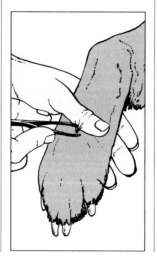

NOSE BLEEDS

These may be caused by trauma or violent sneezing, but are also related in some cases to ulceration of the lining of the nasal cavity. This is a condition more prevalent in German Shepherds than in other breeds.

RECOMMENDED ACTION

1 Keep the dog quiet and use ice packs on the nose.

2 Contact your vet if the bleeding persists.

EYEBALL PROLAPSE

This is not a common problem in German Shepherds, but it may arise from head trauma, e.g. following a dog fight. The eye is forced out of its socket and sight is lost unless it is replaced within fifteen minutes.

RECOMMENDED ACTION

1 Speed is essential. One person should pull the eyelids apart while the other gently presses the eyeball back into its socket, using moist sterile gauze or cloth.

2 If this is impossible, cover the eye with moist sterile gauze and take him to your vet immediately.

GASTRIC DILATION

This is an emergency and cannot be treated at home. The stomach distends with gas and froth which the dog cannot easily eliminate. In some cases, the stomach then rotates and a torsion occurs, so the gases cannot escape at all and the stomach rapidly fills the abdomen. This causes pain, respiratory distress and circulatory failure. Life-threatening shock follows.

PREVENTIVE ACTION

1 Avoid the problem by not exercising your dog vigorously for two hours after a full meal.

2 If your dog is becoming bloated and has difficulty breathing, he is unlikely to survive unless he has veterinary attention within half an hour of the onset of symptoms, so get him to the vet immediately.

POISONING

Dogs can be poisoned by pesticides, herbicides, poisonous plants, paints, antifreeze or an overdose of drugs (animal or human).

■ If poisoning is suspected, first try to determine the agent involved, and find out if it is corrosive or not. This may be indicated on the container, but may also be evident from the blistering of the lips, gums and tongue, and increased salivation.

RECOMMENDED ACTION

■ **CORROSIVE POISONS**

1 Wash the inside of the dog's mouth.

2 Give him milk and bread to protect the gut against the effects of the corrosive.

3 Seek veterinary help.

■ **OTHER POISONS**

1 If the dog is conscious, make him vomit within half an hour of taking the poison.

2 A crystal of washing soda or a few 15ml tablespoonfuls of strong salt solution can be given carefully by mouth.

3 Retain a sample of vomit to aid identification of the poison, or take the poison container with you to show the vet. There may be a specific antidote, and any information can help in treatment.

STINGS

Bee and wasp stings often occur around the head, front limbs or mouth. The dog usually shows sudden pain and paws at, or licks, the stung area. A soft, painful swelling appears; sometimes the dog seems unwell or lethargic. Stings in the mouth and throat can be distressing and dangerous.

RECOMMENDED ACTION

1 Withdraw the sting (bees).

2 Then you can bathe the area in:

■ Vinegar for wasps

■ Bicarbonate for bees

3 An antihistamine injection may be needed.

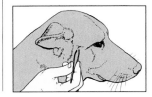

BREEDING

ECLAMPSIA

(See breeding, page 124)
This emergency may occur in your German Shepherd bitch when suckling her puppies, usually when they are about three weeks old.

PARAPHIMOSIS

(See breeding, page 120)
This problem may occur after mating, in the male. The engorged penis is unable to retract into the sheath.

MUZZLING

This will allow a nervous, distressed or injured dog to be examined safely, without the risk of being bitten. A tape or bandage is secured around the muzzle as illustrated. However, a muzzle should not be applied in the following circumstances:

- Airway obstruction
- Loss of consciousness
- Compromised breathing or severe chest injury

1   Tie a knot in the bandage.

2   Wrap around the dog's muzzle with the knot under the lower jaw.

3   Tie firmly behind the dog's head.

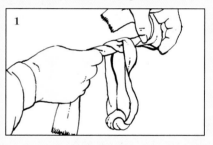

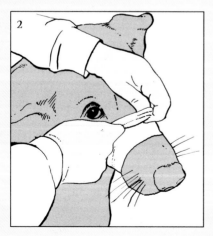

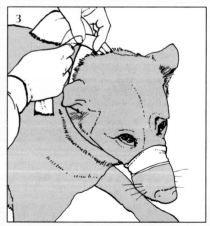

GLOSSARY

Angulation
The angles created by bones meeting at a joint.

Breed standard
The description laid down by the Kennel Club of the perfect breed specimen.

Brood bitch
A female dog which is used for breeding.

Carpals
These are the wrist bones.

Croup
This is the dog's rump: the front of the pelvis to the start of the tail.

Dam
The mother of puppies.

Dew claw
A fifth toe above the ground on the inside of the legs.

Elbow
The joint at the top of the forearm below the upper arm.

Flank
The area between the last rib and hip on the side of the body.

Furnishings
The long hair on the head, legs, thighs, back of buttocks or tail.

Gait
How a dog moves at dfferent speeds.

Guard hairs
Long hairs that grow through the undercoat.

Muzzle
The foreface, or front of the head.

Occiput
The back upper part of the skull.

Oestrus
The periods when a bitch is 'on heat' or 'in season' and responsive to mating.

Pastern
Between the wrist (carpus) and the digits of the forelegs.

Scissor bite
Strong jaws with upper teeth overlapping lower ones.

Stifle
The hind leg joint, or 'knee'.

Undercoat
A dense, short coat hidden below the top-coat.

Whelping
The act of giving birth.

Whelps
Puppies that have not been weaned.

Whiskers
Long hairs on the jaw and muzzle.

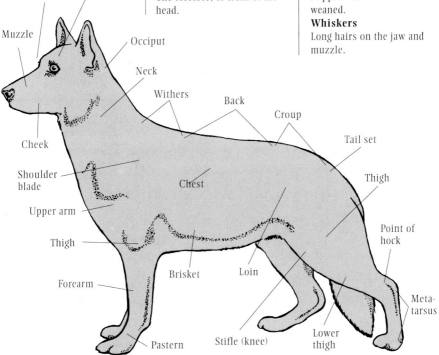

INDEX

USEFUL ADDRESSES

Animal Aunts
Wydnooch,
45 Fairview Rd
Headley Down
Hampshire
GU38 8HQ
(Home sitters,
holidays)

**Animal Studies
Centre,**
Waltham-on-the-Wolds
Melton Mowbray
Leics LE14 4RS
(Animal nutrition)

**Association of Pet
Behaviour
Counsellors**
257 Royal College
Street
London
NW1 9LU

**British Veterinary
Association**
7 Mansfield Street
London W1M 0AT

**Dog Breeders
Insurance Co Ltd**
9 St Stephens Court
St Stephens Road
Bournemouth BH2 6LG
(Books of cover notes
for dog breeders)

**Featherbed
Country Club,**
High Wycombe,
Bucks.
(Luxury dog
accommodation)

**Guide Dogs for the
Blind Association**
Hillfield
Burghfield
Reading
RG7 3YG

**Hearing Dogs for
the Deaf**
The Training Centre
London Road
Lewknor
Oxon OX9 5RY

Home Sitters
Buckland Wharf
Buckland, Aylesbury
Bucks HP22 5LO

The Kennel Club
1-5 Clarges Street,
Piccadilly
London
W1Y 8AB
(Breed Standards,
Breed Club and Field
Trial contact
addresses, registration
forms, Good Citizen
training scheme)

**National Canine
Defence League**
1 & 2 Pratt Mews
London
NW1 0AD

**Pets As Therapy
(PAT Dogs)**
6 New Road, Ditton
Kent ME20 6AD
(Information: how

friendly dogs can join
the hospital visiting
scheme)

**PRO Dogs National
Charity**
4 New Road, Ditton
Kent
ME20 6AD
(Information: Better
British Breeders,
worming certificates to
provide with puppies,
how to cope with grief
on the loss of a loved
dog etc.)

**Royal Society for
the Prevention of
Cruelty to Animals**
RSPCA Headquarters
Causeway
Horsham
West Sussex
RH12 1HG

SCAMPERS SCHOOL FOR DOGS

Scampers helps to train over 200 dogs and puppies every week, using kind, reward-based methods and behaviour therapy, in its unique indoor training facilities. Expert advice is given on all aspects of dog care, and there are puppy, beginners, intermediate and advanced classes. Scampers also run courses for other dog trainers and people interested in a career in dog training.
Scampers Pet Products
This specialist mail order service provides special products, including books, videos, toys, accessories and training equipment, for dog owners. It is based

at Scampers Petcare Superstore, which offers one of the largest ranges of dog accessories in the UK. For more information on Scampers School for Dogs, Scampers Petcare Superstore or Scampers Pet Products contact:

Scampers Petcare Superstore
Northfield Road
Soham
Nr. Ely
Cambs CB7 5UF
Tel: 01353 720431
Fax: 01353 624202